Rust Essentials

Discover how to use Rust to write fast, secure, and concurrent systems and applications

Ivo Balbaert

BIRMINGHAM - MUMBAI

Rust Essentials

First published: May 2015

Production reference: 1220515

Published by Packt Publishing Ltd.
Livery Place
35 Livery Street
Birmingham B3 2PB, UK.

ISBN 978-1-78528-576-9

www.packtpub.com

Credits

Author
Ivo Balbaert

Reviewers
Alfie John
Anthony Miyaguchi
Bharadwaj Srigiriraju
Syed Omar Faruk Towaha
Tony Zou

Commissioning Editor
Akram Hussain

Acquisition Editor
Rebecca Youé

Content Development Editor
Manasi Pandire

Technical Editors
Tanmayee Patil
Shiny Poojary
Mohita Vyas

Copy Editor
Jasmine Nadar

Project Coordinator
Suzanne Coutinho

Proofreaders
Stephen Copestake
Safis Editing

Indexer
Tejal Soni

Production Coordinator
Aparna Bhagat

Cover Work
Aparna Bhagat

About the Author

Ivo Balbaert is currently a lecturer of (web) programming and databases at CVO Antwerpen (www.cvoantwerpen.be), a community college in Belgium. He received a PhD in applied physics from the University of Antwerp in 1986. He worked in the software industry as a developer and consultant for several companies for 20 years and as a project manager at the University Hospital of Antwerp for 10 years. From 2000 onwards, he switched to partly teaching and partly developing software (KHM Mechelen, CVO Antwerp).

He wrote an introductory book in Dutch about developing in Ruby and Rails, *Programmeren met Ruby en Rails, Van Duuren Media*.

In 2012, he authored a book on the Go programming language, *The Way To Go, iUniverse*.

In 2013, in collaboration with Dzenan Ridzanovic, he wrote *Learning Dart* and *Dart Cookbook*, both by Packt Publishing.

In 2014, he wrote *Getting Started with Julia, Packt Publishing*.

I would like to thank the technical reviewers, especially Brian Anderson, Alfie John, and Anne-Marie Mission, for their many useful remarks that improved the text, and my wife, Christiane, for her support.

About the Reviewers

Anthony Miyaguchi is a computer science and engineering student at UCLA. He is active in the open source community and has worked on a variety of different projects, from embedded programming to web technologies. If he finds free time, he would like to make a dent in his collection of books.

Bharadwaj Srigiriraju is a computer science graduate from IIITDM, Jabalpur, who now works as a software developer at Chumbak, Bangalore. He is a technology enthusiast who loves to develop web apps and hack on (shiny) new technologies. He specializes in Python and firmly believes that Rust will replace C very soon. You can reach him at krishna.bharadwaj6@gmail.com or visit his GitHub to know more github.com/bharadwaj6.

Syed Omar Faruk Towaha is a programmer and physicist from Shahjalal University of Science and Technology, Sylhet, Bangladesh. He is involved with the Rust development team and writes and reviews books on several programming languages. He is an Oracle Certified Professional (OCP) developer and loves open source technology. He has been working with several science projects and some research projects at his university as well as in international laboratories. He enjoys designing algorithms and circuit theory. He volunteers at Mozilla by arranging events as a Mozilla representative (http://reps.mozilla.org/).

He is the president of a famous astronomical organization, CAM-SUST (http://camsust.org/). He loves working in teams and being associated with interesting projects.

His recent books include *How You Should Design Algorithms*, *Easy Circuits for Kids*, *Wonder in Quantum Physics*, and *Fundamentals of Ruby*.

You can contact him at soft@hotmail.co.uk. To find out more details about him, go to http://towaha.me/.

I would like to thank the author of this wonderful book and also Suzanne Coutinho and Nikita Michael for their help. This is a pretty good book on Rust, and I will recommend it to anyone who wants to learn Rust. I hope that the author writes more books on Rust, especially by developing games and some exciting things to let the common people know how rich the rust language is.

Tony Zou is currently pursuing his undergraduate studies at the University of Waterloo. He has been programming for 4 years and has worked on a few projects. He enjoys competitive programming and working with exciting new languages such as Rust.

www.PacktPub.com

Support files, eBooks, discount offers, and more

For support files and downloads related to your book, please visit www.PacktPub.com.

Did you know that Packt offers eBook versions of every book published, with PDF and ePub files available? You can upgrade to the eBook version at www.PacktPub.com and as a print book customer, you are entitled to a discount on the eBook copy. Get in touch with us at service@packtpub.com for more details.

At www.PacktPub.com, you can also read a collection of free technical articles, sign up for a range of free newsletters and receive exclusive discounts and offers on Packt books and eBooks.

https://www2.packtpub.com/books/subscription/packtlib

Do you need instant solutions to your IT questions? PacktLib is Packt's online digital book library. Here, you can search, access, and read Packt's entire library of books.

Why subscribe?

- Fully searchable across every book published by Packt
- Copy and paste, print, and bookmark content
- On demand and accessible via a web browser

Free access for Packt account holders

If you have an account with Packt at www.PacktPub.com, you can use this to access PacktLib today and view 9 entirely free books. Simply use your login credentials for immediate access.

Table of Contents

Preface

Rust is the new open source and compiled programming language that finally promises software developers the utmost safety—not only type safety but memory safety as well. The compiler carefully checks all uses of variables and pointers so that common problems from C / C++ and other languages, such as pointers to wrong memory locations or null references, are a thing of the past. Potential problems are detected at compilation time so that Rust programs execute at speeds that are comparable with their C++ counterparts.

Rust runs with a very light runtime, which does not perform garbage collection. Again the compiler takes care of generating code that frees all resources at the right time. This means Rust can run in very constrained environments, such as embedded or real-time systems. When executing code concurrently no data races can occur, because the compiler imposes the same memory safety restrictions as when the code executes consecutively.

From the preceding description, it is clear that Rust is applicable in all use cases where C and C++ were the preferred languages until now and that it will do a better job.

Rust is a very rich language; it has concepts (such as immutability by default) and constructs (such as traits) that enable developers to write code in a highly functional and object-oriented style.

The original goal of Rust was to serve as the language to write a new safe browser engine that was devoid of the many security flaws that plague existing browsers. This is the Servo project from Mozilla Research.

The goal of this book is to give you a firm foundation so that you can start to develop in Rust. Throughout the book, we emphasize the three pillars of Rust: safety, performance, and concurrency. We discuss the areas and the reasons why Rust differs from other programming languages. The code examples are not chosen ad hoc, but they are oriented as part of an ongoing project to build a game so that there is a sense of cohesion and evolution in the examples.

Throughout the book, I will urge you to learn by doing things; you can follow along by typing in the code, making the requested modifications, compiling, testing, and working out the exercises.

What this book covers

Chapter 1, Starting with Rust, discusses the main reasons that led to the development of Rust. We compare Rust with other languages and indicate the areas in which it is most appropriate. Then, we guide you through the installation of all the necessary components for Rust's development environment.

Chapter 2, Using Variables and Types, looks at the basic structure of a Rust program. We discuss the primitive types, how to declare variables and whether they have to be typed, and the scope of variables. Immutability, which is one of the key cornerstones of Rust's safety strategy, is also illustrated. Then, we look at basic operations, how to do formatted printing, and the important difference between expressions and statements.

Chapter 3, Using Functions and Control Structures, shows you how to define functions and the different ways to influence program execution flow in Rust.

Chapter 4, Structuring Data and Matching Patterns, discusses the basic data types for programming, such as strings, vectors, slices, tuples, and enums. Then, we show you the powerful pattern matching that is possible in Rust and how values are extracted by de-structuring patterns.

Chapter 5, Generalizing Code with Higher-order Functions and Parametrization, explores the functional and object-oriented features of Rust. You will see how data structures and functions can be defined in a generic way and how traits can be used to define behavior.

Chapter 6, Pointers and Memory Safety, exposes the borrow checker, which is Rust's mechanism to ensure that only memory safe operations can occur. We discuss different kinds of pointers as well as how to handle runtime errors.

Chapter 7, Organizing Code and Macros, discusses the bigger code-organizing structures in Rust. We will also touch upon how to build macros in order to generate code and save time and effort.

Chapter 8, Concurrency and Parallelism, delves into Rust's concurrency model with its basic concepts of threads and channels. We also discuss a safe strategy for working with shared mutable data.

Chapter 9, Programming at the Boundaries, looks at how Rust can take command-line parameters to process. Then, we go on to look at situations where we have to leave the safety boundaries, such as when we interface with C or use raw pointers, and how Rust minimizes potential dangers when we do so.

Appendix, Exploring Further, talks about the Rust ecosystem and where the reader can find more information about certain topics, such as working with files, databases, games, and web development.

What you need for this book

To run the code examples in the book, you will need the Rust system for your computer, which can be downloaded from `http://www.rust-lang.org/install.html`. This also contains the Cargo project and the package manager. To work more comfortably with the Rust code, a development environment such as Sublime Text can also be of use. *Chapter 1, Starting with Rust*, contains detailed instructions on how to set up your Rust environment.

Who this book is for

This book is intended for developers who have some programming experience in C/C++, Java/C#, Python, Ruby, Dart, or a similar language and a basic knowledge of general programming concepts. It will get you up and running quickly, giving you all you need to start building your own Rust projects.

Conventions

In this book, you will find a number of styles of text that distinguish between different kinds of information. Here are some examples of these styles, and an explanation of their meaning.

Code words in text, database table names, folder names, filenames, file extensions, pathnames, dummy URLs, user input, and Twitter handles are shown as follows: "We can see that `main()` is a function declaration because it is preceded by the keyword `fn`, which is short and elegant like most Rust keywords."

A block of code is set as follows:

```
let tricks = 10;
let reftricks = &mut tricks;
```

When we wish to draw your attention to a particular part of a code block, the relevant lines or items are set in bold:

```
let n1 = {
    let a = 2;
    let b = 5;
    a + b   // <-- no semicolon!
};
```

Any command-line input or output is written as follows:

```
[root]
name = "welcomec"
version = "0.0.1"
```

New terms and **important words** are shown in bold. Words that you see on the screen, in menus or dialog boxes for example, appear in the text like this: "When working with Rust code, select **Tools | Build System | Rust**."

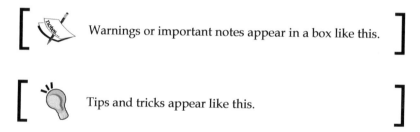

Warnings or important notes appear in a box like this.

Tips and tricks appear like this.

Reader feedback

Feedback from our readers is always welcome. Let us know what you think about this book—what you liked or may have disliked. Reader feedback is important for us to develop titles that you really get the most out of.

To send us general feedback, simply send an e-mail to feedback@packtpub.com, and mention the book title via the subject of your message.

If there is a topic that you have expertise in and you are interested in either writing or contributing to a book, see our author guide on www.packtpub.com/authors.

Customer support

Now that you are the proud owner of a Packt book, we have a number of things to help you to get the most from your purchase.

Downloading the example code

You can download the example code files from your account at http://www. packtpub.com for all the Packt Publishing books you have purchased. If you purchased this book elsewhere, you can visit http://www.packtpub.com/support and register to have the files e-mailed directly to you.

Downloading the color images of this book

We also provide you a PDF file that has color images of the screenshots/diagrams used in this book. The color images will help you better understand the changes in the output. You can download this file from: http://www.packtpub.com/sites/default/files/downloads/14530T_ColorImages.pdf.

Errata

Although we have taken every care to ensure the accuracy of our content, mistakes do happen. If you find a mistake in one of our books—maybe a mistake in the text or the code—we would be grateful if you could report this to us. By doing so, you can save other readers from frustration and help us improve subsequent versions of this book. If you find any errata, please report them by visiting http://www.packtpub.com/submit-errata, selecting your book, clicking on the **Errata Submission Form** link, and entering the details of your errata. Once your errata are verified, your submission will be accepted and the errata will be uploaded to our website or added to any list of existing errata under the Errata section of that title.

To view the previously submitted errata, go to https://www.packtpub.com/books/content/support and enter the name of the book in the search field. The required information will appear under the **Errata** section.

Piracy

Piracy of copyright material on the Internet is an ongoing problem across all media. At Packt, we take the protection of our copyright and licenses very seriously. If you come across any illegal copies of our works, in any form, on the Internet, please provide us with the location address or website name immediately so that we can pursue a remedy.

Please contact us at copyright@packtpub.com with a link to the suspected pirated material.

We appreciate your help in protecting our authors, and our ability to bring you valuable content.

Questions

You can contact us at questions@packtpub.com if you are having a problem with any aspect of the book, and we will do our best to address it.

1
Starting with Rust

Rust is a programming language that is developed by Mozilla Research and backed up by a big open source community. Its development started in 2006 by language designer Graydon Hoare. Mozilla began sponsoring it in 2009, and it was first presented officially in 2010. The work on it went through a lot of iterations, culminating on May 15 2015 with the first stable production version 1.0.0, which was made by the Rust Project Developers who consisted of the Rust team at Mozilla and an open source community of over 900 contributors. Rust is based on clear and solid principles. It is a systems programming language, equaling C and C++ in its capabilities. It rivals idiomatic C++ in speed, but it lets you work in a much safer way by forbidding the use of code that could cause program crashes due to memory problems. Moreover, Rust has the built-in functionality necessary for concurrent execution on multicore machines; it makes concurrent programming memory safe without garbage collection—it is the only language that does this. Rust also eliminates the corruption of shared data through concurrent access, also known as data races.

This chapter will present you with the main reasons why Rust's popularity and adoption are steadily increasing. Then, we'll set up a working Rust development environment.

We will cover the following topics:

- The advantages of Rust
- The trifecta of Rust: safety, speed, and concurrency
- Using Rust
- Installing Rust
- The Rust compiler – `rustc`
- Building our first program
- Working with Cargo
- Developer tools

The advantages of Rust

Mozilla is the company that is known for its mission to develop tools for and drive the evolution of the Web based on open standards, most notably through its flagship browser Firefox. Every browser today, including Firefox, is written in C++ by using some 12,900,992 lines of code for Firefox and 4,490,488 lines of code for Chrome. This enables programs to be fast, but it is inherently unsafe because the memory manipulations allowed by C and C++ are not checked for validity. If the code is written without the utmost programming discipline on the part of the developers, then program crashes, memory leaks, segmentation faults, buffer overflows, and null pointers can occur at program execution. Some of these can result in serious security vulnerabilities, which are all too well-known in existing browsers. Rust is designed from the ground up to avoid these kinds of problems.

On the other side of the programming-language spectrum, we have Haskell, which is widely known to be a very safe and reliable language, but with very little or no control of the level of memory allocation and other hardware resources. We can plot different languages along this control—safety axis, and it seems that when a language is safer, it loses low-level control; the inverse is also true: a language that gives more control over resources provides much less safety, shown as follows:

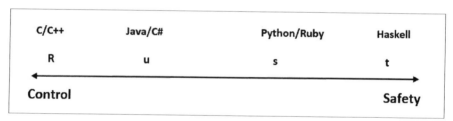

Rust (http://www.rust-lang.org/) is made to overcome this dilemma by providing the following features:

- High safety through its strong type system
- Deep but safe control over low-level resources (as much as C/C++) so that it runs close to the hardware

Rust lets you specify exactly how your values should be laid out in memory and how that memory should be managed; this is why it works well at both ends of the control and safety line. This is the unique selling point of Rust: it breaks the safety-control dichotomy that, before Rust, existed in programming languages. With Rust, control and safety can be achieved together without losing performance.

Rust can accomplish both these goals without a garbage collector, in contrast to most modern languages such as Java, C#, Python, Ruby, Go; in fact Rust doesn't even have a garbage collector yet (though one is planned). Rust is a compiled language: the strict safety rules are enforced by the compiler so that they do not cause runtime overhead. As a consequence, Rust can work with minimal runtime or even no runtime at all; so, it can be used for real time or embedded projects, and it can easily integrate with other languages or projects.

Rust is meant for developers and projects where not only performance and low-level optimizations are important, but where there is also a need for a safe and stable execution environment. Moreover, Rust adds a lot of high-level functional programming techniques within the language so that it feels like a low-level and a high-level language at the same time.

The trifecta of Rust – safety, speed, and concurrency

Rust is not a revolutionary language with new cutting-edge features, but it incorporates a lot of proven techniques from older languages while massively improving upon the design of C++ in matters of safe programming.

The Rust developers designed Rust to be a general-purpose and multi-paradigm language. Like C++, it is an imperative, structured, and object-oriented language. Besides this, it inherits a lot from functional languages and also incorporates advanced techniques for concurrent programming.

In Rust, the typing of variables is static (because Rust is compiled) and strong. However, unlike Java or C++, the developer is not forced to indicate the types for everything as the Rust compiler is able to infer the types in many cases.

C and C++ are known to be haunted by a series of problems that often lead to program crashes or memory leaks which are notoriously difficult to debug and solve. Think about dangling pointers, buffer overflows, null pointers, segmentation faults, data races, and so on. The Rust compiler (called `rustc`) is very intelligent and can detect all these problems while compiling your code, thereby guaranteeing memory safety during execution. This is done by the compiler by retaining complete control over memory layout, without needing the runtime burden of garbage collection (see *Chapter 6, Pointers and Memory Safety*). In addition, its safety also implies much less possibilities for security breaches.

Rust compiles native code like Go and Julia. However, in contrast to these two, Rust doesn't need runtime with garbage collection. In this respect, it also differs from Java JVM and the languages that run on the JVM, such as Scala and Clojure. Most other popular modern languages such as .NET with C# and F#, JavaScript, Python, Ruby, Dart, and so on, all need a virtual machine and garbage collection.

As one of its mechanisms for concurrency, Rust adopts the well-known actor model from Erlang. Lightweight processes called threads perform work in parallel. They do not share heap memory but communicate data through channels, and data races are eliminated by the type system (see *Chapter 8, Concurrency and Parallelism*). These primitives make it easy for programmers to leverage the power of many CPU cores that are available on current and future computing platforms.

The `rustc` compiler is completely self hosted, which means that it is written in Rust and can compile itself by using a previous version. It uses the LLVM compiler framework as its backend (for more information on LLVM compiler framework, go to `http://en.wikipedia.org/wiki/LLVM`) and produces natively executable code that runs blazingly fast because it compiles to the same low-level code as C++ (To see an example of its speed, go to `http://benchmarksgame.alioth.debian.org/u64q/rust.php.`).

Rust is designed to be as portable as C++ and run on widely used hardware and software platforms; at present, it runs on Linux, Mac OS X, Windows, FreeBSD, Android, and iOS. It can call C's code as simply and efficiently as C can call its own code, and conversely, C can also call Rust code (see *Chapter 9, Programming at the Boundaries*). The following is the logo of Rust:

Other Rust characteristics that will be discussed in more detail in later chapters are as follows:

- Its variables are immutable by default (see *Chapter 2, Using Variables and Types*)
- Enums (see *Chapter 4, Structuring Data and Matching Patterns*)
- Pattern matching (see *Chapter 4, Structuring Data and Matching Patterns*)

- Generics (see *Chapter 5, Generalizing Code with Higher-order Functions and Parametrization*)
- Higher-order functions and closures (see *Chapter 5, Generalizing Code with Higher-order Functions and Parametrization*)
- The interface system called traits (see *Chapter 5, Generalizing Code with Higher-order Functions and Parametrization*)
- A hygienic macro system (see *Chapter 7, Organizing Code and Macros*)
- Zero-cost abstractions, which means that Rust has higher-language constructs, but these do not have an impact on performance

In conclusion, Rust gives you ultimate power over memory allocation as well as removing many security and stability problems that are commonly associated with native languages.

Comparison with other languages

Dynamic languages such as Ruby or Python give you the initial coding speed, but you pay the price later when you have to write more tests, runtime crashes, or even production outages. The Rust compiler forces you to get a lot of things right at compile-time, which is the least expensive place to identify and fix bugs.

Rust's object orientation is not that explicit or evolved as common object-oriented languages such as Java, C#, and Python as it doesn't have classes. Compared with Go, Rust gives you more control over memory and resources, so lets you code on a lower level. Go also works with a garbage collector, and it has no generics or a mechanism to prevent data races between its goroutines that are used in concurrency. Julia is focused on numerical computing performance; it works with a JIT compiler and doesn't give you that low-level control that Rust gives.

Using Rust

It is clear from the previous sections that Rust can be used in projects that normally use C or C++. Indeed, many regard Rust as a successor or a replacement of C and C++. Although Rust is designed to be a systems language, it has a broad range of possible applications due to its richness of constructs, making it an ideal candidate for applications that fall into one or all of the following categories:

- Client applications, such as browsers
- Low-latency, high-performance systems, such as device drivers, games, and signal processing
- Highly distributed and concurrent systems, such as server applications

- Real-time and critical systems, such as operating systems or kernels

- Embedded systems (that require a very minimal runtime footprint) or a resource-constrained environment, such as a Raspberry Pi, Arduino, or robotics

- Tools or services that can't support the long warm-up delays that are common in **Just In Time (JIT)** compiler systems and need instantaneous startup

- Web frameworks

- Large-scale, high-performance, resource intensive, and complex software systems

Rust is especially suited when code quality is important, that is for:

- Modestly-sized or larger developer teams

- Code for long-running production use

- Code with a longer lifetime that requires regular maintenance and refactoring

- Code for which you would normally write a lot of unit tests to safeguard it

Even before the appearance of Rust 1.0, two companies already use it in production:

- OpenDNS (`http://labs.opendns.com/2013/10/04/zeromq-helping-us-block-malicious-domains/`) is a middleware tool for blocking malware and malicious domains

- Skylight (`https://www.skylight.io/`) from the company Tilde (`http://www.tilde.io/`) is a tool for monitoring the execution of Rails apps.

Servo

Mozilla uses Rust as the language for writing Servo, its new web browser engine that is designed for parallelism and safety (`https://github.com/servo/servo`).

Due to the design of Rust's compiler, many kinds of browser security bugs are prevented automatically. In 2013, Samsung got involved, porting Servo to Android and ARM processors. Servo itself is an open source project with more than 200 contributors. It is under heavy development, and among other things, it has already implemented its own CSS3 and HTML5 parser in Rust. It passed the web compatibility browser test ACID2 in March 2014 (`http://en.wikipedia.org/wiki/Acid2/`).

Installing Rust

The Rust compiler and tools can be downloaded from `http://www.rust-lang.org/install.html` in the binary (that is, executable) form. The platform comes for the three major operating systems (Linux 2.6.18 or a later version, OS X 10.7 or a later version, and Windows 7, Windows 8, and Windows Server 2008 R2) in both the 32- and 64-bit formats, and it is delivered as an installer or in an archive format. You should use the current official stable release 1.0 when you engage in professional work with Rust. If you would like to investigate or use the latest developments, install the nightly build version.

For Windows, double-click on the `.exe` installer to install the Rust binaries and dependencies. Adding Rust's directory to the search path for executables is an optional part of the installation, so make sure that this option is selected.

For Linux and Mac OS X, the simplest way is to run the following command in your shell:

```
curl -sSL https://static.rust-lang.org/rustup.sh | sh
```

Verify the correctness of the installation by showing Rust's version with `rustc -V` or `rustc - -version`, which produces an output like `rustc 1.0.0-beta (9854143cb 2015-04-02) (built 2015-04-02)`.

Rust can be uninstalled by running `C:\Rust\unins001.exe` on Windows or `/usr/local/lib/rustlib/uninstall.sh` on Linux.

Rust has also been ported to Android OS on ARM processors and iOS.

A bare metal stack called zinc for running Rust in embedded environments can be found at `http://zinc.rs/`. However, at this moment, only the ARM architecture is supported by it.

The source code resides on GitHub (`https://github.com/rust-lang/rust/`) and if you want to build Rust from source, we refer you to `https://github.com/rust-lang/rust#building-from-source`.

The Rust compiler – rustc

The Rust installation directory containing `rustc` can be found on your machine in the following folder:

- In Windows, at `C:\Program Files\Rust 1.0\bin` or a folder of your choice
- On Linux or Mac OS X, it can be found by navigating to `/usr/local/bin`

If the Rust home folder was added to the search path for executables, `rustc` can be run from any command-line window. The Rust libraries can be found in the `rustlib` subfolder of the `bin` directory on Windows, or in `/usr/local/lib/rustlib` on Linux. Its HTML documentation can be found at `C:\Rust\share\doc\rust\html` on Windows or `/usr/local/share/doc/html` on Linux.

The `rustc` command has the following format: `rustc [options] input`.

The options are one letter directives for the compiler after a dash, such as `-g` or `-W`, or words prefixed by a double dash, such as `--test` or `--no-analysis`. All the options with some explanation are shown when invoking `rustc -h`. In the next section, we will verify our installation by compiling and running our first Rust program.

Our first program

Let's get started by showing a welcome message to the players of our game:

1. Open your favorite text editor (such as notepad or gedit) for a new file and type in the following code:

    ```
    // code in Chapter1\code\welcome.rs
    fn main() {
        println!("Welcome to the Game!");
    }
    ```

2. Save the file as `welcome.rs`.

    `rs` is the standard extension of Rust code files. Source file names may not contain spaces; if they contain more than one word, use an underscore `_` as a separator; for example, `start_game.rs`.

3. Then, compile it to native code on the command line with the following:

    ```
    rustc welcome.rs
    ```

    This produces an executable program `welcome.exe` on Windows or `welcome` on Linux.

4. Run this program with `welcome` or `./welcome` to get the following output:

    ```
    Welcome to the Game!
    ```

The output executable gets its name from the source file. If you want to give the executable another name, such as `start`, compile it with the `-o output_name` option:

```
rustc welcome.rs -o start
```

The `rustc -O` command produces a native code that is optimized for execution speed (which is equivalent to `rustc -C opt-level=2`; the most optimized code is generated for `rustc -C opt-level = 3`).

Compiling and running are separate, consecutive steps, contrary to dynamic languages such as Ruby or Python where these are performed in one step.

Let's explain the code a bit to you. If you have already worked in a C/Java/C# like environment, this code will seem quite familiar. As in most languages, execution of the code starts in a `main()` function, which is mandatory in an executable program.

In a larger project with many source files, the file containing the `main()` function would be called `main.rs` by convention.

We can see that `main()` is a function declaration because it is preceded by the keyword `fn`, which is short and elegant like most Rust keywords. `()` after main denotes the parameter list, which is empty here. The function's code is placed in a code block, which is surrounded by curly braces (`{ }`) where the opening brace is put by convention on the same line as the function declaration, but it is separated by one space. The closing brace appears after the code here, right beneath `fn`.

Our program has only one line, which is indented by four spaces to improve readability (Rust is not whitespace sensitive). This line prints the string, "Welcome to the Game!". Rust recognizes this as a string because it is surrounded by double quotes (`" "`). This string was given as an argument to the `println!` macro (`!` indicates that it is a macro and not a function). The code line ends with a semicolon (`;`), as most, but not all, code lines in Rust do (see *Chapter 2, Using Variables and Types*).

Perform the following exercises:

- Write, compile, and execute a Rust program `name.rs` that prints out your name.
- What is the smallest possible program in Rust in terms of code size?

The `println!` macro has some nice formatting capabilities and at the same time checks when compiling whether the type of variables is correct for the applied formatting (see *Chapter 2, Using Variables and Types*).

Working with Cargo

Cargo is Rust's package and dependency manager, and it is similar to Bundler, npm, pub, or pip for other languages. Although you can write Rust programs without it, Cargo is nearly indispensable for any large project; it works the same whether you work on a Windows, Linux, or a Mac OS X system. The installation procedure from the previous section includes the Cargo tool, so Rust is shipped with tooling included.

Cargo does the following things for you:

- It makes a tidy folder structure and some templates for your project with the `cargo new` command
- It compiles (builds) your code by using the `cargo build` command
- It runs your project by using `cargo run`
- If your project contains unit tests, it can execute them for you by using `cargo test`
- If your project depends on packages, it will download them and build these packages according to the needs of your code by using `cargo update`

We'll introduce how to use Cargo now, and we'll come back to it later, but you can find more info here: `http://doc.crates.io/guide.html`.

Let's remake our first project `welcomec` using Cargo by performing the following steps:

1. Start a new project `welcomec` using the following command:

   ```
   cargo new welcomec --bin
   ```

   The `--bin` option tells Cargo that we want to make an executable program (a binary). This creates the following directory structure:

   ```
   ivo@ubuntu:~/Rust_Book$ cd welcomec
   ivo@ubuntu:~/Rust_Book/welcomec$ tree .
   .
   ├── Cargo.toml
   └── src
       └── main.rs

   1 directory, 2 files
   ivo@ubuntu:~/Rust_Book/welcomec$
   ```

   A folder with the same name as the project is created; in this folder, you can put all kinds of general information such as a `License` file, a README file, and so on. In addition, a `src` subfolder is created that contains a template source file named `main.rs`. (This contains the same code as our `welcome.rs` file, but it prints out the string "Hello world!".)

The file `Cargo.toml` (with capital C) is the configuration file or manifest of your project; it contains all the metadata that Cargo needs to compile your project. It follows the so-called TOML format (for more details about this format, go to `https://github.com/toml-lang/toml`) and contains the following text with information about our project:

```
[package]
name = "welcomec"
version = "0.0.1"
authors = ["Your name <you@example.com>"]"
```

This file is editable, so other sections can be added. For example, you can add a section to tell Cargo that we want a binary with the name welcome:

```
[[bin]]
name = "welcome"
```

2. We can build our project (no matter how many source files it contains) using the following command:

```
cargo build
```

This gives us the following output (on Linux):

```
Compiling welcomec v0.0.1 (file:///home/ivo/Rust_Book/
welcomec)
```

Now, the following folder structure is produced:

The directory target contains the executable `welcome`.

3. To execute this program, run the following command:

```
cargo run
```

This produces the following output:

```
Running `target/welcome`
Hello, world!
```

Step 2 has also produced a file named `Cargo.lock`; this is used by Cargo to keep track of dependencies in your application. At the moment, the application only contains:

```
[root]
name = "welcomec"
version = "0.0.1"
```

The same file format is used to lock down the versions of libraries or packages that your project depends on. If your project is built in the future when updated versions of the libraries are available, Cargo will make sure that only the versions recorded in `Cargo.lock` are used so that your project is not built with an incompatible version of a library. This ensures a repeatable build process.

Perform the following exercise:

- Make, build, and run a project `name` that prints out your name with Cargo.

The website at `https://crates.io/` is the central repository for Rust packages or crates (as they are called) and contained 1700 crates as of the end of March 2015. You can search for crates using specific terms or browse them alphabetically or according to the number of downloads:

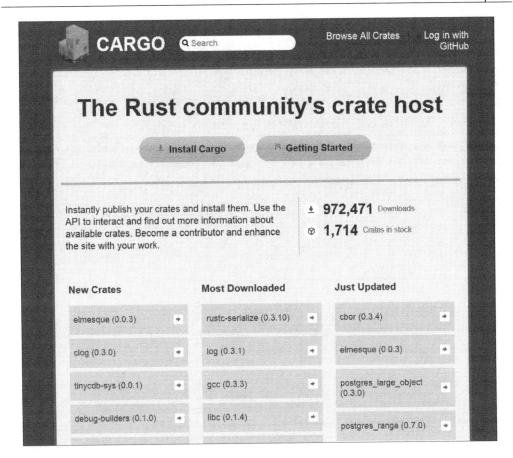

The developer tools

Since Rust is a systems programming language, the only thing that you need is a good text editor (but not a word processor!) for writing the source code, and everything else can be done by commands in a terminal session. However, some developers appreciate the functionalities offered by more fully fledged text editors which are specifically for programming or IDE's (short for integrated development environments). Rust is still young but a lot of possibilities have already come up on this front although some of them need to be updated in the latest Rust version.

Rust plugins exist for a host of text editors, such as Atom, Brackets, BBEdit, Emacs, Geany, GEdit, Kate, TextMate, Textadept, Vim, NEdit, Notepad++, and SublimeText. Most Rust developers work with Vim or Emacs. These come with a syntax highlighting, and code completion tool called racer; go to `https://github.com/phildawes/racer`.

Using Sublime Text

The plugins for the popular Sublime Text editor (http://www.sublimetext.com/3) are particularly pleasant to work with, and they don't get in your way. After you have installed Sublime Text (you might want to get a registered version), you must also install the Package Control package. (For instructions on how to do this, go to https://packagecontrol.io/installation).

Then, to install the Sublime Text Rust plugin, open the palette in Sublime Text (*Ctrl + Shift + P* or *cmd + Shift + P* on Mac OS X) and select **Package Control | Install Package**. Then, select **Rust** from the list, you will see something like the following screenshot:

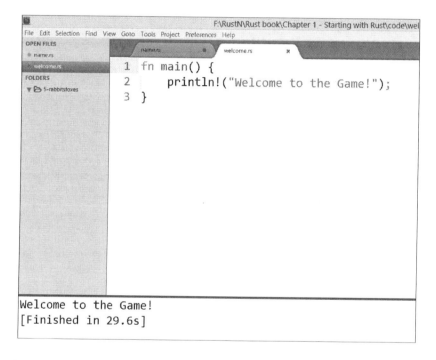

Sublime Text is a very comprehensive text editor, which includes color schemes. The Rust plugin provides syntax highlighting and auto-completion. Type one or more letters, choose an option from the list that appears with an arrow key and press *Tab* to insert the code snippet, or simply select a list-option through a mouse click. To compile and execute Rust code, follow these steps:

1. Mark **Tools | Build System | Rust** in the menu.
2. Then, you can compile a source file by pressing *Ctrl + B*. Warnings or errors will appear in the lower pane; if everything is okay, a message similar to **[Finished in 0.6s]** will appear.

3. Then, you can run the program by pressing *Ctrl + Shift + B*; again the output will appear beneath the code. Alternatively, you can use the menu items: **Tools | Build** and **Tools | Run**.

A SublimeLinter plugin exists that provides an interface to rustc, which is called `SublimeLinter-contrib-rustc`. It does additional checks on your code for stylistic or programming errors. You can install it, as explained earlier, through Package Control and then use it from the menu **Tools | SublimeLinter**. (For more details, go to `https://github.com/oschwald/SublimeLinter-contrib-rustc`.) There is also a code completion tool called *racer*; you can find the information on how to install it at `https://packagecontrol.io/packages/RustAutoComplete`.

Other tools

RustDT (`http://rustdt.github.io/`) is a new and promising Rust IDE based on Eclipse. On top of all the editing functionality offered by Eclipse, it is project-based using Cargo. Moreover it has code completion and debugging functionality (using the GDB debugger).

There are also plugins such as the following ones for IDEs at different states of completion:

- The *RustyCage* plugin (`https://github.com/reidarsollid/RustyCage`) for Eclipse
- The *idea-rust* plugin (`http://plugins.jetbrains.com/plugin/7438`) for IntelliJ
- The *rust-netbeans* plugin (`https://github.com/azazar/rust-netbeans`) for NetBeans
- The *VisualRust* plugin (*https://github.com/PistonDevelopers/VisualRust*) for Visual Studio

You can test out the Rust code even without local installation with the Rust Play Pen: `http://play.rust-lang.org/`. Here you can edit or paste your code, and evaluate it.

The *rusti* is an interactive shell or **Read-Evaluate-Print-Loop** (**REPL**) that is being developed for Rust; this is common for dynamic languages, but it is remarkable for a statically compiled language. You can find it at `https://github.com/murarth/rusti`.

Summary

In this chapter, we gave you an overview of Rust's characteristics, where Rust can be applied, and compared it to other languages. We made our first program, demonstrated how to build a project with Cargo, and gave you choices to make a more complete development environment.

In the next chapter, we look at variables and types and explore the important concept of mutability.

2
Using Variables and Types

In this chapter, we look at the basic building blocks of a Rust program: variables and their types. We discuss variables of primitive types, whether their type has to be declared or not, and the scope of variables. Immutability, one of the cornerstones of Rust's safety strategy, is also discussed and illustrated.

We will cover the following topics:

- Comments
- Global constants
- Values and primitive types
- Binding variables to values
- Scope of a variable and shadowing
- Type checking and conversions
- Expressions
- The stack and the heap

Our code examples will center on building a text-based game called Monster Attack.

Comments

Ideally, a program should be self-documenting by using descriptive variable names and easy to read code, but there are always cases where additional comments about a program's structure or algorithms are needed. Rust follows the C convention and has the following convention for marking comments:

- **Line comments** (//): Everything on the line after // is commentary and not compiled
- **Block or multi-line comments** (/* */): Everything between the start /* and the end */ is not compiled

However, the preferred Rust style is to use only line comments even for multiple lines, like the following code:

```
// see Chapter 2/code/comments.rs
fn main() {
  // Here starts the execution of the Game.
  // We begin with printing a welcome message:
  println!("Welcome to the Game!");
}
```

Use the block comments only to comment out code.

Rust also has a doc comment (///) that is useful in larger projects that require an official documentation for customers and developers. Such comments have to appear before an item (like a function) on a separate line to document that item. In these comments, you can use Markdown formatting syntax; for more information, go to https://en.wikipedia.org/wiki/Markdown.

Here is a doc comment:

```
/// Start of the Game
fn main() {
}
```

We'll see more relevant uses of doc comments in later code snippets. The rustdoc tool can compile these comments into a project's documentation.

Global constants

Often, an application needs a few values that are in fact constants; they do not change in the course of the program. For example: the name of our game, which is "Monster Attack", is a constant, as is the maximum value of health, which is the number 100. We must be able to use them in main() or any other function in our program, so they are placed at the top of the code file. They live in the global scope of the program. Such constants are declared with the static keyword as follows:

```
// see Chapter 2/code/constants1.rs
static MAX_HEALTH: i32 = 100;
static GAME_NAME: &'static str = "Monster Attack";

fn main() {
}
```

Names of constants must be in uppercase and underscores can be used to separate words. Their type must also be indicated; MAX_HEALTH is a 32-bit integer (i32) and GAME_NAME is a string (str). As we will discuss further, the declaration of types for variables is done in exactly the same way although this is often optional when the compiler can infer the type from the code's context.

Don't worry too much about the &'static indication for now. Remember that Rust is a low-level language, so many things must be specified in detail. The & annotation is a reference to something (it contains the memory address of a value); here it contains the reference to the string. However, if we only use &str and compile, we get an error for that line. Have a look at the following snippet:

```
// warning: incorrect code!
static GAME_NAME: &str = "Monster Attack";
```

This will give you the following error:

2:22 error: missing lifetime specifier [E0106]

Here, 2:22 means that we have an error on line 2 and position 22, so we must set the line numbering in our editor. We must add the lifetime specifier 'static to the type annotation so that we get &'static str. The lifetime of an object in Rust is very important because it says how long the object will live in the program's memory. The Rust compiler adds the code to remove an object when its lifetime is over, freeing the memory that it occupied. The 'static lifetime is the longest possible lifetime; such an object stays alive throughout the entire application, and so it is available to all of its code.

Even when we add this specifier, the compiler gives us the warning: static item is never used: `MAX_HEALTH`, #[warn(dead_code)] on by default warning and an analogous warning for GAME_NAME.

These warnings do not prevent the compilation, so at this stage, we have an executable. However, the compiler is right. These objects are never used in the program's code; so, in a complete program, you should either use them or throw them out.

It takes a while before an aspiring Rust developer starts to regard the Rust compiler as his or her friend and not an annoying machine that keeps spitting out errors and warnings. As long as you see this message at the end of the compiler output, `error: aborting due to previous errors`, no (new) executable is made. But remember, correcting the errors eliminates runtime problems, so this can save you a lot of time that would be otherwise wasted tracking nasty bugs. Often, the error messages are accompanied with helpful notes on how to eliminate the error. Even the warnings can point you to flaws in your code. Rust also warns us when something is declared but not used in the code that follows, such as unused variables, functions, imported modules, and so on. It even warns us if we make a variable mutable (which means that its value can be changed) when it should not be or when code doesn't get executed. The compiler does such a good job that when you reach the stage where all errors and warnings are eliminated, your program will most likely run correctly!

Besides static values, we can also use simple constant values whose value never changes. Constants always have to be typed, for example, `const PI: f32 = 3.14;` they are more local in scope than static values.

The compiler automatically substitutes the value of the constant everywhere in the code.

Printing with string interpolation

An obvious way to use variables is to print out their values, as we have done here:

```
// see Chapter 2/code/constants2.rs
static MAX_HEALTH: i32 = 100;
static GAME_NAME: &'static str = "Monster Attack";

fn main() {
  const PI: f32 = 3.14;
  println!("The Game you are playing is called {}.", GAME_NAME);
  println!("You start with {} health points.", MAX_HEALTH);
}
```

This gives the following output:

```
The Game you are playing is called Monster Attack.
You start with 100 health points.
```

The constant PI exists in the standard library, to use this value insert this statement at the top: use `std::f32::consts;` and then use the PI value as follows: `println!("{}", consts::PI);`

The first argument of `println!` is a literal format string that contains a `{}` placeholder. The value of the constant or variable after the comma is converted to a string and replaces the `{}`. There can be more than one placeholder, and they can be numbered in order so that they can be used repeatedly, as shown in the following code:

```
println!("In the Game {0} you start with {1} % health, yes you read it
correctly: {1} points!", GAME_NAME, MAX_HEALTH);
```

The output is as follows:

```
In the Game Monster Attack you start with 100 % health, yes you read it
correctly: 100 points!
```

The placeholder can also contain one or more named arguments, as follows:

```
println!("You have {points} % health", points=70);
```

This will give you the following output:

```
You have 70 % health
```

Special ways of formatting can be indicated inside `{}` after a colon (`:`), as follows:

```
println!("MAX_HEALTH is {:x} in hexadecimal", MAX_HEALTH); // 64
println!("MAX_HEALTH is {:b} in binary", MAX_HEALTH);   // 1100100
println!("pi is {:e} in floating point notation", PI); // 3.14e0
```

The following formatting possibilities exist according to the type that must be printed:

- o for octal
- x for lower hexadecimal
- X for upper hexadecimal
- p for a pointer
- b for binary
- e for lower exponential notation
- E for upper exponential notation
- ? for debugging purposes

The `format!` macro has the same parameters and works in the same way as `println!`, but it returns a string instead of printing out.

Go to `http://doc.rust-lang.org/std/fmt/` for an overview of all the possibilities.

Values and primitive types

Constants that have been initialized have a value. Values exist in different types: 70 is an integer, 3.14 is a float, and z and θ are of the char type (they are characters). Characters are unicode values that take 4 bytes of memory each. Godzilla is a string of type &str (which is a Unicode UTF8 by default), true and false are of the bool type; they are Boolean values. Integers can be written in different formats:

- Hexadecimal format with 0x (for example, 0x46 for 70)
- Octal format with 0o, (for example, 0o106 for 70)
- Binary format with 0b, (for example, 0b1000110)

Underscores can be used for readability, as in 1_000_000. Sometimes, the compiler will urge you to indicate more explicitly the type of number with a suffix. For example, the number after u or i is the number of memory bits used, namely 8, 16, 32, or 64:

- 10usize denotes an unsigned integer of machine word size usize, which can be any of the u8, u16, u32, or u64 types
- 10isize denotes a signed integer of machine word size isize, which can be any of the types among i8, i16, i32, and i64
- In the preceding cases, for a 64-bit operating system usize is in fact u64 and isize is equivalent to i64
- 3.14f32 denotes a 32-bit floating point number
- 3.14f64 denotes a 64-bit floating point number

The numeric types i32 and f64 are the defaults if no suffix is given, but in that case, to differentiate between them, you must end an f64 value with .0, like this: let e = 7.0;.

Indicating a specific type is only needed when the compiler signals that it cannot infer the type of the variable.

Rust is like any other C-like language when it comes to the different operators that exist on values and their precedence (go to http://doc.rust-lang.org/reference.html#binary-operator-expressions for more information on this). However, note that Rust does not have increment (++) or decrement (--) operators. To compare two values for equality, use == and to test whether they are different use !=.

There is even the empty value () of zero size, which is the only value of the so-called unit type (). This is used to indicate the return value when an expression or a function returns nothing (no value), as is the case for a function that only prints to the console. () is not the equivalent of a null value in other languages; () means no value, whereas null is a value.

Consulting Rust documentation

The quickest way to find more detailed information about a Rust topic is to browse the documentation screen of the standard library at http://doc.rust-lang.org/std/. On its left-hand side, you can find a listing of all the available crates that you can browse for more details. However, the most useful feature is the search box at the top; you can type in a few letters or a word to get a number of useful references. Have a look at the following screenshot:

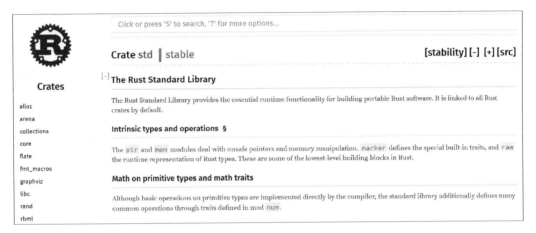

The following is an exercise for you:

- Try to change the value of a constant. This is of course not allowed. What error do you get? Have a look at Chapter2/exercises/change_constant.rs.

- Look up the println! macro in the documentation.

- Read the fmt specification and write a program that will print the 3.2f32 value as +003.20. Refer to Chapter2/exercises/formatting.rs.

Binding variables to values

Storing all values in constants is not an option. It is not good because constants live as long as the program and therefore be changed, and often we want to change values. In Rust, we can bind a value to a variable by using a let binding:

```
// see Chapter 2/code/bindings.rs
fn main() {
   let energy = 5; // value 5 is bound to variable energy
}
```

Unlike many other languages such as Python or Go, the semicolon (;) is needed here to end the statement. Otherwise, the compiler will throw the `error: expected one of \`.\`, \`;\`, or an operator, found \`}\`` error at us.

We also want to create bindings only when they are used in the rest of the program, but you needn't worry because the Rust compiler warns us about that:

```
values.rs:2:6: 2:7 warning: unused variable: `energy`, #[warn(unused_
variables)] on by default
```

 For prototyping purposes, you can suppress the warning by prefixing the variable name with a _ , like in `let _ energy = 5;`. In general, _ is used for variables that we don't need.

Note that in the preceding declaration, we didn't need to indicate the type; Rust inferred the type of `energy` to be an integer, which the `let` binding triggered. If the type is not obvious, the compiler searches in the code context to check from where the variable gets a value or how it is used.

However, giving type hints like `let energy = 5u16;` is also okay; this way you help the compiler a bit by indicating the type of energy, which is a 2-byte unsigned integer in this case.

We can use the `energy` variable by using it in an expression; for example, by assigning it to another variable or by printing it:

```
let copy_energy = energy;
println!("Your energy is {}", energy););
```

Here are some other declarations:

```
let level_title = "Level 1";
let dead = false;
let magic_number = 3.14f32;
let empty = ();  // the value of the unit type ()
```

The value of `magic_number` could also be written as `3.14_f32`; the _ separates the digits from the type to improve readability.

Declarations can replace previous declarations of the same variable. A statement like `let energy = "Abundant";` would now bind energy to the value Abundant of string type. The old declaration can no longer be used and its memory is freed.

Mutable and immutable variables

Suppose we get a boost from swallowing a health pack and our energy rises to value 25. However, if we write energy = 25;, we get an error: re-assignment of immutable variable `energy` error. So, what is wrong here?

Well, Rust applies a programmer's wisdom here; a lot of bugs come from inadvertent or wrong changes made to variables, so don't let the code change a value unless you have deliberately allowed it!

 Variables are by default **immutable** in Rust, which is very similar to what functional languages do. In pure functional languages, mutability is not even allowed.

If you want a mutable variable because its value can change during code execution, you have to indicate that explicitly with mut. Have a look at the following code snippet:

```
let mut fuel = 34;
fuel = 60;
```

Simply declaring a variable as let n; is also not enough. If we do this, we will get error: unable to infer enough type information about `_`; type annotations required. The compiler needs a value to infer its type.

We can give the compiler this information by assigning a value to n, like n = -2;, but as the message says, we could also indicate its type as follows:

```
let n: i32;
```

Alternatively, you can even use the following:

```
let n: i32 = -2; // n is a binding of type i32 and value -2
```

The type (here i32) follows the variable name after a colon (:) (as we already showed for global constants), optionally followed by an initialization. In general, the type is indicated like n: T, where n is a variable and T is a type, and it is read as variable n is of the type T. So, this is the inverse of what is done in C/C++, Java, or C#, where one would write T n.

For primitive types, this can be done simply with a suffix, like this:

```
let x = 42u8;
let magic_number = 3.14f64;
```

Trying to use an uninitialized variable results in the `error: use of possibly uninitialized variable` error (try it out). Local variables have to be initialized before they can be used in order to prevent undefined behavior.

You can experiment with a mutable global constant. What do you have to do to allow it? Why would that be? (For an example code, see `mutable_constant.rs`.)

When the compiler does not recognize a name in your code, you will get an `unresolved name` error. This may probably be just a typo, but it will be caught early on at compilation and not at runtime!

Scope of a variable and shadowing

All variables defined in `bindings.rs` have local scope delimited by `{ }` of the function, which happens to be `main()` here, and this applies to any function. After the ending `}`, they go out of scope and their memory allocation is freed.

We can even make a more limited scope inside a function by defining a code block that contains all the code within a pair of curly braces (`{ }`), as in the following snippet:

```
// see Chapter 2/code/scope.rs
fn main() {
  let outer = 42;
  { // start of code block
      let inner = 3.14;
      println!("block variable: {}", inner);
      let outer = 99; // shadows the first outer variable
      println!("block variable outer: {}", outer);
  } // end of code block
    println!("outer variable: {}", outer);
  }
```

This gives the following output:

```
block variable: 3.14
block variable outer: 99
outer variable: 42
```

A variable defined in the block (like `inner`) is only known inside that block. A variable in the block can also have the same name as a variable in an enclosing scope (like `outer`), which is replaced (shadowed) by the block variable until the block ends. What do you think will happen when you try to print `inner` after the block? Try it out.

So, why would you want to use a code block? In the *Expressions* section, we will see that a code block can return a value that can be bound to a variable with let. A code block can also be empty ({   }).

Type checking and conversions

Rust has to know the type of each variable so that it can check (at compile time) whether they are only used in the manner in which their type permits. This way programs are type safe and a whole range of bugs can be avoided.

This also means that we cannot change the type of a variable during its lifetime because of static typing; for example, the score variable in the following snippet cannot change from an integer to a string:

```
// see Chapter 2/code/type_errors.rs
// warning: this code does not work!
fn main() {
  let score: i32 = 100;
  score = "YOU WON!"
}
```

We get the compiler error, error: mismatched types: expected `int`, found `&'static str` (expected int, found &-ptr.

However, we are allowed to write the following code:

```
let score = "YOU WON!";
```

Rust lets us redefine variables; each let binding creates a new variable score that hides the previous one, which is freed from memory. This is actually quite useful because variables are immutable by default.

Adding strings with + (like the players in the following code) is not defined in Rust:

```
let player1 = "Rob";
let player2 = "Jane";
let player3 = player1 + player2;
```

We then get error: binary operation `+` cannot be applied to type `&str`.

In Rust, you can use the to_string() method to convert the value to a String type like this: let player3 = player1.to_string() + player2;.

Otherwise, you could use the format! macro:

```
let player3 = format!("{}{}", player1, player2);
```

In both the cases, `player3` has the value `"RobJane"`.

Let's find out what happens when you assign a value from a variable of a certain type to another variable of a different type:

```
// see Chapter 2/code/type_conversions.rs
fn main() {
    let points = 10i32;
    let mut saved_points: u32 = 0;
    saved_points = points; // error !
}
```

This is again not allowed; we get the same error (error: `mismatched types: expected `u32`, found `i32`` (expected u32, found i32)). To enable maximal type checking, Rust does not permit automatic (or implicit) conversions of one type to another like C++ does; therefore, it avoids a lot of hard-to-find bugs. For example, the numbers after the decimal point are lost when a `f32` value is converted to an `i32` value; this could lead to errors when done automatically.

We can, however, do an explicit conversion (a casting) with the `as` keyword:

```
saved_points = points as u32;
```

When points contain a negative value, the sign would be lost after conversion. Similarly, when casting from a wider value like a float to an integer, the decimal part is truncated:

```
let f2 = 3.14;
saved_points = f2 as u32; // truncation to value 3 occurs here
```

In addition, the value must be convertible to the new type as a string cannot be converted to an integer, as shown in the following example:

```
let mag = "Gandalf";
saved_points = mag as u32; // error: non-scalar cast:`&str`as`u32`
```

Aliasing

It can be useful sometimes to give a new, more descriptive or a shorter name to an existing type. This can be done with the `type` keyword, as in the following example where we needed a specific (but size-limited) variable for `MagicPower`:

```
// see Chapter 2/code/alias.rs
type MagicPower = u16;

fn main() {
    let run: MagicPower= 7800;
}
```

A type name starts with a capital letter, as does each word that is part of the name. What happens when we change the value 7800 to 78000? The compiler detects this with the following warning, `warning: literal out of range for its type`.

Expressions

Rust is an **expression-oriented** language, which means that most pieces of code are in fact expressions, that is, they compute a value and return that value (in that sense, values are also expressions). However, expressions by themselves do not form meaningful code; they must be used in statements.

The `let` bindings like the following are declaration statements; they are not expressions:

```
// see Chapter 2/code/expressions.rs
let a = 2;     // a binds to 2
let b = 5;     // b binds to 5
let n = a + b;   // n binds to 7
```

However, `a + b` is an expression, and if we omit the semicolon at the end, the resulting value (here 7) is returned. This is often used when a function needs to return its value (see examples in the next chapter). Ending an expression with a semicolon like `a + b;` suppresses the value of an expression, thereby throwing away the return value and making it an expression statement that returns the unit value `()`. A code is usually a sequence of statements, one on each code line, and Rust has to know when a statement ends; this is why nearly every Rust code line ends with a semicolon.

What do you think the assignment `m = 42;` is? This is not a binding because there is no `let`. That should have happened on a previous code line. It is an expression that returns the unit value `()`. A compound binding like `let p = q = 3;` is not allowed in Rust; it returns the `error: unresolved name q` error. However, you can chain `let` bindings like this:

```
let mut n = 0;
let mut m = 1;
let t = m; m = n; n  = t;
println!("{} {} {}", n, m, t); // which prints out 1 0 1
```

Here is an exercise for you. Print out the values of a, b, and n after this code snippet and explain the value of a (for example code, see `compound_let.rs`):

```
let mut a = 5;
let mut b = 6;
let n = 7;
let a = b = n;
```

A code block is also an expression, which will return the value of its last expression if we omit the semicolon. For example, in the following code snippet, `n1` gets the value 7, but `n2` gets no value (or rather the unit value `()`) because the return value of the second code block was suppressed:

```
let n1 = {
    let a = 2;
    let b = 5;
    a + b    // <-- no semicolon!
};
    println!("n1 is: {}", n1);   // prints: n1 is 7

    let n2 = {
      let a = 2;
      let b = 5;
      a + b;
    };
    println!("n2 is: {:?}", n2);   // prints: n2 is ()
```

Here, the variables `a` and `b` are declared in a code block and live only as long as the block itself lives as they are local to the block. Note that the semicolon after the closing brace of the block (`};`) is needed. To print the unit value `()`, we need `{:?}` as the format specifier.

The stack and the heap

Since memory allocation is very important in Rust, we must have a good picture of what is going on. A program's memory is divided into the stack and heap memory parts; to get more background on these concepts, read the information on the classic web page at https://stackoverflow.com/questions/79923/what-and-where-are-the-stack-and-heap. Primitive values such as numbers (like 32 in the figure), characters, and true/false values are stored on the stack, while the value of more complex objects that could grow in size are stored in the heap memory. Heap values are referenced by a variable on the stack, which contains the memory address of the object on the heap:

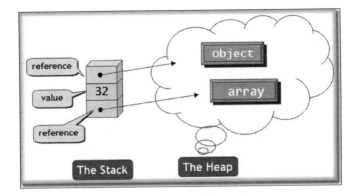

While the stack has a limited size, the size of the heap can grow as and when more space is needed.

Now, we will run the following program and try to visualize the program's memory:

```
// see Chapter 2/code/references.rs
let health = 32;
let mut game = "Space Invaders";
```

Values are stored in memory and so they have memory addresses. The health variable contains an integer value 32 that is stored in the stack at location 0x23fba4, while the variable game contains a string, which is stored in the heap starting at location 0x23fb90. (These were the addresses when I executed the program, but they will be different when you run the program.)

The variables to which the values are bound are pointers or references to the values. They point to them; game is a reference to Space Invaders. The address of a value is given by the & operator. So, &health is the address where value 32 is stored, and &game is the address where the Space Invaders' value is stored.

We can print these addresses by using the format string {:p} for pointers like this:

```
println!("address of health-value: {:p}", &health);
// prints 0x23fba4
println!("address of game-value: {:p}", &game); // prints 0x23fb90
println!("game-value: {}", game); // prints "Space Invaders"
```

Now, we have the following situation in memory (memory addresses will be different at each execution):

	memory location	name	value
H	0x23fb90		"Space Invaders"
E			
A			
P			
S			
T	0x23fba4		32
A	0x08	health	0x23fba4
C	0x04	game	0x23fb90
K		game2	0x23fb90

We can make an alias, which is another reference that points to the same place in memory, like this:

```
let game2 = &game;
println!("{:p}", game2); // prints 0x23fb90
```

To get the value that is being referred to rather than the `game2` reference itself, dereference it with the asterisk `*` operator like this:

```
println!("{}", *game2); // prints "Space Invaders"
```

The (`println!` is clever, so `println!("{}", game2);` line will also print the same value as `println!("game: {}", &game);`.

The preceding code is a bit simplified because Rust will allocate values to the stack that will not change in size as much as it is possible, but this is meant to give you a better idea of what a reference to a value means.

We know already that a `let` binding is immutable, so the value cannot be changed:

```
health = 33; // error: re-assignment of immutable variable `health`.
```

If `y` is declared with `let y = &health;`, then `*y` is the value 32. Reference variables can also be given a type like `let x: &i64;` and such references can be passed around in code. After this `let` binding, `x` does not really point yet to a value and it does not contain a memory address. In Rust, there is no way to create a null pointer as you can in other languages; if you try to assign a nil, null, or even a unit value `()` to x, this will result in an error. This feature alone saves Rust programmers from countless bugs. Furthermore, trying to use x in an expression; for example, `println!("{:?}", x);` will result in the `error: use of possibly uninitialized variable: `x`error` error.

A mutable reference to an immutable variable is forbidden; otherwise, the immutable variable could be changed through its mutable reference:

```
let tricks = 10;
let reftricks = &mut tricks;
```

This gives the `error: cannot borrow immutable local variable `tricks` as mutable` error.

A reference to a mutable score variable can either be immutable or mutable respectively, such as `score2` and `score3` in the following example:

```
let mut score = 0;
let score2 = &score;
// error: cannot assign to immutable borrowed content *score2
// *score2 = 5;

let mut score = 0;
let score3 = &mut score;
  *score3 = 5;
```

The value of `score` can be only changed through a mutable reference such as `score3`.

For reasons that we will see later, you can only make one mutable reference to a mutable variable:

```
let score4 = &mut score;
```

This throws the `error: cannot borrow `score` as mutable more than once at a time` error.

Here, we touch the heart of Rust's memory safety system, where borrowing a variable is one of its key concepts. We will explore this in more detail in *Chapter 6, Pointers and Memory Safety*.

The heap is a much larger memory part than the stack, so it is important that memory locations are freed as soon as they are no longer needed. The Rust compiler sees when a variable ends its lifetime (or in other words, goes out of scope) and inserts a code at compile time to free its memory when the code is executed. This behavior is unique to Rust and is not present in other commonly used languages. Stack values can be boxed, that is, allocated in the heap by creating a `Box` around them, as is the case for the value of x in the following code:

```
let x = Box::new(5i32);
```

`Box` is an object that references a value on the heap. We'll also look at this more closely in the *Boxes* section of *Chapter 6, Pointers and Memory Safety*.

Summary

In this chapter, you learned how to work with variables in Rust and got acquainted with many of the common compiler error messages. We explored types and the default immutability of variables that are the cornerstones of Rust's safety behavior. In the following chapter, we will start writing some useful code by using program logic and functions.

3
Using Functions and Control Structures

This chapter concentrates on how we can control the execution flow of our code and modularize our code through functions. We will also learn how to get input from the console, and how to document and test our code.

We will cover the following topics:

- Branching on a condition
- Looping
- Functions
- Attributes
- Testing

Branching on a condition

Branching on a condition is done with a common `if`, `if-else`, or `if-else if-else` construct, as shown in this example:

```
// from Chapter 3/code/ifelse.rs
fn main() {
  let dead = false;
  let health = 48;
  if dead {
    println!("Game over!");
    return;
  }
  if dead {
    println!("Game over!");
```

```
      return;
   } else {
      println!("You still have a chance to win!");
   }
   if health >= 50 {
      println!("Continue to fight!");
   } else if health >= 20  {
      println!("Stop the battle and gain strength!");
   } else {
      println!("Hide and try to recover!");
   }
}
```

This gives the following output:

```
Stop the battle and gain strength!
```

The condition after if has to be a Boolean. However, unlike in C, the condition must not be enclosed within parentheses. Code blocks surrounded by { } (curly braces) are needed after if, else if, or else. The first example shows that we can get out of a function with return.

Another feature of if-else, as it is an expression, is that it returns a value. This value can be used as a function call parameter in a print! statement, or it can be assigned to a let binding like this:

```
let active =
if health >= 50 {
    true
} else {
    false
};
println!("Am I active? {}", active);
```

The output is as follows:

```
Am I active? false
```

The code blocks can contain many lines. However, you need to be careful when you return a value to ensure that you omit ; (the semicolon) after the last expression in the if or else block. (For more information on this, see the *Expressions* section of *Chapter 2, Using Variables and Types*). Moreover, all branches must always return a value of the same type. This alleviates the need for a ternary operator (? :) that is needed in C++; you can simply use if as follows:

```
let adult = true;
let age = if adult { "+18" } else { "-18" };
println!("Age is {}", age);   // Age is +18
```

As an exercise, try the following:

1. Try adding a ; (semi-colon) after +18 and -18, like this {"+18";} and find out what value will be printed for age. What happens if you type annotate age as &str?

2. See whether you can omit { } (the curly braces) if there is only one statement in the block.

3. Also, verify whether this code is okay:

   ```
   let result = if health <=0 { "Game over man!" };
   ```

   How would you correct this statement, if necessary? (Refer to code in Chapter 3/exercises/iftest.rs.)

4. Simplify the following function:

   ```
   fn verbose(x: i32) -> &'static str {
       let mut result: &'static str;
       if x < 10 {
           result = "less than 10";
       } else {
           result = "10 or more";
       }
       return result;
   }
   ```

   (See the code in Chapter 3\exercises\ifreturn.rs.)

Pattern matching, which we will examine in the next chapter, also branches code, but it does this based on the value of a variable.

Looping

For repeating pieces of code, Rust has the common while loop, again without parentheses around the condition:

```
// from Chapter 3/code/loops.rs
fn main() {
    let max_power = 10;
    let mut power = 1;
    while power < max_power {
        print!("{} ", power); // prints without newline
        power += 1;            // increment counter
    }
}
```

This prints the following output:

```
1 2 3 4 5 6 7 8 9
```

To start an infinite loop, use `loop`, which is syntactic sugar for while true:

```
loop {
  power += 1;
  if power == 42 {
    // Skip the rest of this iteration
    continue;
  }
  print!("{}  ", power);
  if power == 50 {
    print!("OK, that's enough for today");
    break;  // exit the loop
  }
}
```

Here, all power values including 50 are printed; then the loop stops with `break`. However, the power value 42 is not printed because of the `continue` statement. So, loop is equivalent to a while true, and a loop with a conditioned break simulates a do while in other languages.

When loops are nested inside each other, break and continue apply to the immediate enclosing loop. Any `loop` statement (also `while` and `for` that we'll see next) can be preceded by a label (which is denoted as `'label:`) to allow us to jump to the next or outer enclosing loop, as shown in this code snippet:

```
'outer: loop {
    println!("Entered the outer dungeon - ");
    'inner: loop {
        println!("Entered the inner dungeon - ");
        // break;     // this would break out of the inner loop
        break 'outer; // breaks to the outer loop
    }
    println!("This treasure can sadly never be reached - ");
}
println!("Exited the outer dungeon!");
```

The code prints the following output:

```
Entered the outer dungeon -
Entered the inner dungeon -
Exited the outer dungeon!
```

The infamous `goto` from C does not exist in Rust!

Looping where a `var` variable begins from a start value `a` to an end value `b` (exclusive) is done with `for` over a range expression `for var in a..b` statement. Here is an example that prints the squares of the numbers from 1 to 10:

```
for n in 1..11 {
        println!("The square of {} is {}", n, n * n);
}
```

In general, `for in` loops over an iterator, which is an object that gives back a series of values one by one. The range `a..b` is the simplest form of iterator. Each subsequent value is bound to n and used in the next loop iteration. The `for` loop ends when there are no more values, and n then goes out of scope. If we don't need the value of n in the loop, we can replace it with _ (an underscore) like this: `for _ in 1..11 { }`.The many bugs in the C-style `for` loops, like the off-by-one error with the counter, cannot occur here because we loop over an iterator.

Variables can also be used in a range, like in the following snippet that prints nine dots:

```
let mut x = 10;
for _ in 1 .. x { x -= 1; print!("."); }
```

We'll examine iterators in more detail in *Chapter 5, Generalizing Code with Higher-order Functions and Parametrization*.

Functions

The starting point of every Rust program is a `fn` function called `main()`, which can be further subdivided into separate functions to reuse code or for better code organization. Rust doesn't care about the order in which these functions are defined, but it is nice to put `main()` at the start of the code to get a better overview. Rust has incorporated many features of traditional functional languages; we will see examples of this in *Chapter 5, Generalizing Code with Higher-order Functions and Parametrization*.

Let's start with an example of a basic function:

```
// from Chapter 3/code/functions.rs
fn main() {
    let hero1 = "Pac Man";
    let hero2 = "Riddick";
    greet(hero2);
    greet_both(hero1, hero2);
}
```

```
fn greet(name: &str) {
    println!("Hi mighty {}, what brings you here?", name);
}

fn greet_both(name1: &str, name2: &str) {
    greet(name1);
    greet(name2);
}
```

The output is as follows:

```
Hi mighty Riddick, what brings you here?
Hi mighty Pac Man, what brings you here?
Hi mighty Riddick, what brings you here?
```

Like variables, functions also have snake_case names that must be unique, and their parameters (which have to be typed) are separated by commas. In this code snippet, the examples are name1: &str and name2: &str (it looks like a binding, but without let).

Mandating a type to the parameters was an excellent design decision: this documents the function for use by its caller code and allows type inference inside the function. The type here is &str because strings are stored on the heap (see the *The stack and the heap* section of *Chapter 2, Using Variables and Types*).

The functions in the preceding code don't return anything useful (in fact, they return the unit value ()), but if we want a function to actually return a value, its type must be specified after an arrow(->), as shown in this example:

```
fn increment_power(power: i32) -> i32 {
    println!("My power is going to increase:");
    power + 1
}

fn main() {
    let power = increment_power(1); // function is called
    println!("My power level is now: {}", power);}
}
```

When executed this prints the following:

```
My power is going to increase:
I am now at power level: 2
```

The return value of a function is the value of its last expression. Note that in order to return a value, the final expression must not end with a semicolon. What happens when you do end it with a semicolon? Try this out. In this case, the unit value () will be returned, and the compiler will give you the error, **not all control paths return a value error**.

We could have written return power + 1; as the last line, but this is not idiomatic code. If we wanted to return a value from the function before the last code line, we have to write a return value; as shown in here:

```
if power < 100 { return 999; }
```

If this was the last line in the function, you would write it like this:

```
if power < 100 { 999 }
```

A function can return only one value, but this isn't a limitation. If we have, for example, three values a, b, and c to return, make one tuple (a, b, c) with them and return this. We will examine tuples in more detail in the next chapter. In Rust, you can also write a function inside another function (a so-called nested function), contrary to C or Java. However, this should only be used for small helper functions that are needed locally.

The following is an exercise for you:

What is wrong with the following function that returns the absolute value of a given number x?

```
fn abs(x: i32) -> i32 {
   if x > 0 {
      x
   } else {
      -x
   }
}
```

You need to correct and test it. (See the code in Chapter 3/exercises/absolute.rs.)

Documenting a function

Let's show you an example of documentation. In exdoc.rs, we have documented a cube function as follows:

```
fn main() {
   println!("The cube of 4 is {}", cube(4));
}
/// Calculates the cube `val * val * val`.
///
```

```
///  # Examples
///
///  ```
///  let cube = cube(val);
///  ```
pub  fn  cube(val:  u32)  -> u32  {
     val  *  val  *  val
}
```

If we now invoke `rustdoc exdoc.rs` on the command line, a `doc` folder will be created. This contains an `exdoc` subfolder with `index.html` that is the starting point of a website that provides a documentation page for each function. For example, `fn.cube.html` shows the following:

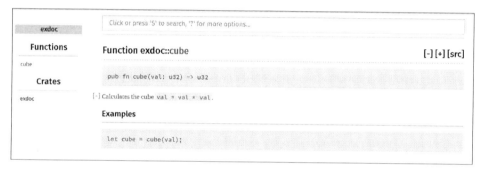

By clicking on the **exdoc** link, you can return to the index page. For a project that is made with the cargo package manager, issue the `cargo doc` command to obtain its documentation.

Documentation comments are written in markdown. They can contain the following special sections preceded by #: Examples, Panics, Failures, and Safety. A code appears between ```. For a function to be documented, it must be prefixed with `pub` so that it belongs to the public interface (see *Chapter 7, Organizing Code and Macros*). For more information on this, go to `http://doc.rust-lang.org/book/documentation.html`.

Attributes

You may have already seen examples of warnings within #[...] signs, such as #[warn(unused_variables)], in compiler output. These are **attributes** that represent **metadata** information about the code and are placed right before an item (such as a function) about which they have something to say. They can, for example, disable certain classes of warnings, turn on certain compiler features, or mark functions as being part of unit-tests or benchmark code.

Conditional compilation

If you want to make a function that only works on a specific operating system then annotate it with the #[cfg(target_os = "xyz")] attribute (where xyz can be either windows, macos, linux, android, freebsd, dragonfly, bitrig, or openbsd). For example, the following code works fine and runs on Windows:

```
// from Chapter 3/code/attributes_cfg.rs
fn main() {
  on_windows();
}

#[cfg(target_os = "windows")]
fn on_windows() {
    println!("This machine has Windows as its OS.")
}
```

This produces the output, **This machine has Windows as its OS**. If we try to build this code on a Linux machine, we get the **error: unresolved name `on_windows`** error, as the code does not build on Linux because the attribute prevents it from doing so!

Furthermore, you can even make your own custom conditions; go to http://rustbyexample.com/attribute/cfg/custom.html for more information on this.

Attributes are also used when testing and benchmarking code.

Testing

We can prefix a function with the #[test] attribute to indicate that it is part of the unit tests for our application or library. We can then compile with rustc --test program.rs. This will replace the main() function with a test runner and show the result from the functions marked with #[test]. Have a look at the following code snippet:

```
// from Chapter 3/code/attributes_testing.rs
fn main() {
println!("No tests are compiled,compile with rustc --test! ");
}

#[test]
fn arithmetic() {
  if 2 + 3 == 5 {
    println!("You can calculate!");
  }
}
```

Test functions, such as `arithmetic()` in the example, are black boxes; they have no arguments or returns. When this program is run on the command line, it produces the following output:

```
running 1 test
test arithmetic ... ok

test result: ok. 1 passed; 0 failed; 0 ignored; 0 measured
```

However, even if we change the test to `if 2 + 3 == 6`, the test passes! Try it out. It turns out that test functions always pass when their execution does not cause a crash (called a panic in Rust terminology), and it fails when it does panic. This is why testing (or debugging) uses the `assert_eq!` macro (or other similar macros):

```
assert_eq!(2, power);
```

This statement tests whether `power` has the value 2. If it does, nothing happens, but if `power` is different from 2, an exception occurs and the program panics with, **thread '<main>' panicked at 'assertion failed**.

In our first function, we will write the `assert_eq!(5, 2 + 3);` test that will pass. We can also write this as `assert!(2 + 3 == 5);` by using the `assert!` macro.

A test fails when the function panics, as is the case with the following example:

```
#[test]
fn badtest() {
    assert_eq!(6, 2 + 3);
}
```

This produces the following output:

```
failures:
    badtest

test result: FAILED. 1 passed; 1 failed; 0 ignored; 0 measured

thread '<main>' panicked at 'Some tests failed', C:\bot\slave\nightly-dist-rustc-
win-64\build\src\libtest\lib.rs:265
```

Unit test your functions by comparing the actual function result to the expected result with an `assert_eq!(actual, expected)` macro call. In a real project, the tests will be collected in a separate tests module. (Have a look at *Chapter 7, Organizing Code and Macros*, for more information.)

Testing with cargo

An executable project, or a crate as it is called in Rust, needs to have a main() startup function, but a library crate, to be used in other crates, does not need a main() function. Create a new mylib library crate with cargo as cargo new mylib.

This creates a src subfolder with a lib.rs source file that contains the following code:

```
#[test]
fn it_works() {
}
```

So a library crate is created with no code of its own, but it does contain a test template to augment with the unit tests that you write on the functions of your library. You can then run these tests with cargo test, which will produce an output similar to that produced in the previous section. The cargo test command runs tests in parallel whenever it is possible.

Summary

In this chapter, you learned how to make basic programs by using the if conditions, while and for loops, and functions to structure our code. We were also able to accept input to a program. Lastly, we saw the immense power that attributes give to widen Rust's possibilities, and we applied this in conditional compilation and testing.

In the next chapter, we will start using composite values and explore the powers of pattern matching.

4
Structuring Data and Matching Patterns

Until now we have only used simple data, but to do real programming, more composite and structured data values are needed. Among them are flexible arrays and tuples, enums, and structs that represent more object-like behavior, similar to that found in classical object-oriented languages. Options are another important type that are used to ensure that cases where no value is returned are accounted for. Then, we will look at pattern matching, which is another typical functional construct in Rust. However, we will start by looking more carefully at strings. We will cover the following topics:

- Strings
- Arrays, vectors, and slices
- Tuples
- Structs
- Enums
- Getting input from the console
- Matching patterns

Strings

The way Rust works with strings differs a bit to how strings work in other languages. All strings are valid sequences of Unicode (UTF-8) bytes. They can contain null bytes, but they are not null terminated as in C. Rust distinguishes two types of strings:

- Literal strings, which we have used until now, are string slices whose type is &str. The & character points out that the string slice is a reference to a string. They are immutable and have a fixed size. For example, the following bindings declare string slices:

```
// from Chapter 4/code/strings.rs
    let magician1 = "Merlin";
    let greeting = "Hello, 世界!";
```

  Otherwise, we care to explicitly annotate the string variable with its type:

```
let magician2: &'static str = "Gandalf";
```

  The &'static command denotes that the string is statically allocated. We saw this notation earlier in *Chapter 2, Using Variables and Types*, when we declared global string constants. In that case, indicating the type was mandatory, but for a let binding, it is superfluous because the compiler infers the type:

```
println!("Magician {} greets magician {} with {}",
        magician1, magician2, greeting);
```

  Prints out: `Magician Merlin greets magician Gandalf with Hello, 世界!`

  These strings live as long as the program; they have the lifetime of the program, which is the static lifetime. They are described in the std::str module.

- A String on the other hand can grow dynamically in size (it is in fact a buffer), and so it must be allocated on the heap. We can create an empty string with the following snippet:

```
let mut str1 = String::new();
```

  Each time the string grows, it has to be reallocated in the memory. So, for example, if you know that it will start out as 25 bytes , you can create the string by allocating this amount of memory as follows:

```
let mut str2 = String::with_capacity(25);
```

This type is described in the `std::string` module. To convert a string slice into a String, use the `to_string` method:

```
let mut str3 = magician1.to_string();
```

The `to_string()` method can be used to convert any object into a `String` (more precisely, any object that implements the `ToString` trait; we will talk about traits in the next chapter). This method allocates memory on the heap.

If `str3` is a String, then you can make a string slice from it with `&str3` or `&str3[..]`:

```
let sl1 = &str3;
```

A string slice created this way can be considered as a view into the `String`. It is a reference to the interior of the String and making it has no cost involved.

I prefer this way instead of `to_string()` when comparing strings because using `&[..]` doesn't consume resources while `to_string()` allocates heap memory:

```
if &str3[] == magician1 {
    println!("We got the same magician alright!")
}
```

To build a String, we can use a number of methods, which are as follows:

- The `push` method: This appends a character to the String
- The `push_str` method: This appends another string to the String

You can see them in action in the following code snippet:

```
let c1 = 'θ';   // character c1
str1.push(c1);
println!("{}", str1); // θ
str1.push_str(" Level 1 is finished - ");
println!("{}", str1); // θ Level 1 is finished -
str1.push_str("Rise up to Level 2");
println!("{}", str1); // θ Level 1 is finished - Rise up to Level 2
```

If you need to get the characters of a `String` one by one and in order, use the `chars()` method. This method returns an `Iterator`, so we can use the for in loop (see the *Looping* section of *Chapter 2, Using Variables and Types*):

```
for c in magician1.chars() {
    print!("{} - ", c);
}
```

Which prints out: M - e - r - l - i - n -.

To loop over the parts of a String that are separated by whitespace, we can use the split() method, which also returns an Iterator:

```
for word in str1.split(" ") {
    print!("{} / ", word);
}
```

Which prints out: 0 / Level / 1 / is / finished / - / Rise / up / to / Level / 2 /.

To change the first part of a String that matches with another string, use the replace method:

```
let str5 = str1.replace("Level", "Floor");
```

This code allocates new memory for the modified str5 string.

When you write a function that takes a string as an argument, always declare it as a string slice, which is a view into the string, as shown in the following code snippet:

```
fn how_long(s: &str) -> usize { s.len() }
```

The reason for this is that passing a String str1 as argument allocates memory, so we better pass it as a slice. The easiest and most elegant way to do this is as follows:

```
println!("Length of str1: {}", how_long(&str1));
```

Or:

```
println!("Length of str1: {}", how_long(&str1[..]));
```

Consult the documentation at http://doc.rust-lang.org/std/str/ and http://doc.rust-lang.org/std/string/ for more functionality. Here is a schema to see the difference between the two string types more clearly:

String	String slice (&str)
mutable – heap memory allocation	fixed size – static lifetime – view on String – reference(&)
module: std::string	module: std::str

Arrays, vectors, and slices

Suppose we have a bunch of alien creatures to populate a game level, then we would probably want to store their names in a handy list. Rust's array is just what we need:

```
// from Chapter 4/code/arrays.rs
let aliens = ["Cherfer", "Fynock", "Shirack", "Zuxu"];
println!("{:?}", aliens);
```

To make an array, separate the different items by commas and enclose the whole thing within [ ] (rectangular brackets). All the items must be of the same type. Such an array must be of a fixed size (this must be known at compile time) and cannot be changed; this is stored in one contiguous piece of memory.

If the items have to be modifiable, declare your array with `let mut`; however, even then the number of items cannot change. The aliens array could be of the type that is annotated as `[&str; 4]` where the first parameter is the type of the items and the second is their number:

```
let aliens: [&str; 4] = ["Cherfer", "Fynock", "Shirack", "Zuxu"];
```

If we want to initialize an array with three Zuxus, that's easy too:

```
let zuxus = ["Zuxu"; 3];
```

How would you then make an empty array? This is shown as follows:

```
let mut empty: [i32; 0] = [];
println!("{:?}", empty); // []
```

We can also access individual items with their index, starting from 0:

```
println!("The first item is: {}", aliens[0]); // Cherfer
println!("The third item is: {}", aliens[2]); // Shirack
```

The number of items in the array is given by `aliens.len()`; so, how would you get the last item? Exactly! By using `aliens[aliens.len() - 1]`. Alternatively, this can be found by using `aliens.iter().last().unwrap();`.

Pointers to arrays use automatic dereferencing so that you do not need to use `*` explicitly, as demonstrated in this code snippet:

```
let pa = &aliens;
println!("Third item via pointer: {}", pa[2]);
```

Which prints: `Third item via pointer: Shirack`. What do you think will happen when we try to change an item as follows:

```
aliens[2] = "Facehugger";
```

Hopefully, you didn't think that Rust would allow this, did you? Unless you told it explicitly that aliens can change with `let mut aliens = [...]`; then it is alright!

The index is also checked at runtime to be within the array bounds of 0 and `aliens.len()`; if it is not, the program will crash with a runtime error or panic:

```
println!("This item does not exist: {}", aliens[10]);
// runtime error:
```

It gives the following output:

```
thread '<main>' panicked at 'index out of bounds: the len is 4 but the
index is 10'
```

If we want to go through the items successively one by one and print them out or do something useful with them, we can do it as follows:

```
for ix in 0..aliens.len() {
    println!("Alien no {} is {}", ix, aliens[ix]);
}
```

This works and it gives us the index for each item, which might be useful. However, when we use the index to fetch each consecutive item, Rust also has to check each time whether we are still within the bounds of the array in memory. That's why this is not very efficient, and in the *Iterators* section of *Chapter 5, Generalizing Code with Higher-order Functions and Parametrization*, we will see a much more efficient way by iterating over the items as follows:

```
for a in aliens.iter() {
    println!("The next alien is {}", a);
}
```

The `for` loop can be written even shorter as follows:

```
for a in &aliens  { … }
```

Vectors

Often, it is more practical to work with a kind of array that can grow (or shrink) in size because it is allocated on the heap. Rust provides this through the `Vec` vector type from the `std::vec` module. This is a generic type, which means that the items can have any `T` type, where `T` is specified in the code; for example, we can have vectors of the `Vec<i32>` type or the `Vec<&str>` type. To indicate that this is of the generic type, it is written as `Vec<T>`. Again, all elements must be of the same `T` type. We can make a vector in two ways, with `new()` or with the `vec!` macro. These are shown here:

```
let mut numbers: Vec<i32> = Vec::new();
let mut magic_numbers = vec![7i32, 42, 47, 45, 54];
```

In the first case, the type is indicated explicitly with `Vec<i32>`; in the second case, this is done by giving the first item an `i32` suffix, but this is usually optional.

We can also make a new vector and allocate an initial memory size to it, which can be useful if you know in advance that you will need at least that many items. The following initializes a vector for signed integers with a memory allocated for 25 integers:

```
let mut ids: Vec<i32> = Vec::with_capacity(25);
```

We need to provide the type here, otherwise the compiler would not be able to calculate the amount of memory needed.

A vector can also be constructed from an iterator through the `collect()` method with a range, such as in this example:

```
let rgvec: Vec<u32> = (0..7).collect();
println!("Collected the range into: {:?}", rgvec);
```

which prints out: `Collected the range into: [0, 1, 2, 3, 4, 5, 6].`

Indexing, getting the length, and looping over a vector works the same as with arrays. For example, a `for` loop over a vector can be written simply as follows:

```
let values = vec![1, 2, 3];
for n in values {
        println!("{}", n);
}
```

Add a new item to the end of a vector with `push()`, remove the last item with `pop()`:

```
numbers.push(magic_numbers[1]);
numbers.push(magic_numbers[4]);
println!("{:?}", numbers); // [42, 54]
let fifty_four = numbers.pop();// fifty_four now contains 54
println!("{:?}", numbers); // [42]
```

If a function needs to return many values of the same type, you can make an array or vector with these values and return that object.

Slices

What would you do if you want to do something with a part of an array or a vector? Perhaps, your first idea is to copy that part out to another array, but Rust has a safer and more efficient solution; take a slice of the array. No copy is needed, instead you get a view into the existing array, similar to how a string slice is a view into a string.

As an example, suppose I only need the numbers 42, 47, and 45 from our `magic_numbers` vector. Then, I can take the following slice:

```
let slc = &magic_numbers[1..4]; // only the items 42, 47 and 45
```

The starting index 1 is the index of 42, the last index 4 points to 54, but this item is not included. The `&` shows that we are referencing an existing memory allocation. Slices share the following with vectors:

- They are generic and have the `&[T]` type for a `T` type
- Their size does not have to be known at compile time

Strings and arrays

Back in the first section of this chapter, we saw that the sequence of characters in a `String` is given by the `chars()` function. Doesn't this look like an array to you? A `String` is backed up by an array if we look at the memory allocation of its characters; it is stored as a vector of bytes `Vec<u8>`.

This means that we can also take a slice of the `&str` type from a `String`:

```
let location = "Middle-Earth";
let part = &location[7..12];
println!("{}", part); // Earth
```

We can collect the characters of a slice into a vector and sort them as follows:

```
let magician = "Merlin";
let mut chars: Vec<char> = magician.chars().collect();
chars.sort();
for c in chars.iter() {
    print!("{} ", c);
}
```

This prints out `M e i l n r` (capital letters come before small letters in the sort order). Here are some other examples of using the `collect()` method:

```
let v: Vec<&str> = "The wizard of Oz".split(' ').collect();
let v: Vec<&str> = "abc1def2ghi".split(|c: char| c.is_numeric()).
collect();
```

Here, `split()` takes a closure to determine on which character to split. Both the slice types, `&str` and `&[T]`, can be seen as views into `String`s and vectors respectively. The following scheme compares the types that we just encountered (`T` denotes a generic type):

Fixed-size (stack allocated)	Slices		Dynamic size (growable) (heap allocated)
	`&str` type: `&[u8]`	is a view into	`String`
array type: `[T;size]`	slice type: `&[T]`	is a view into	Vector type: `Vec<T>`

Perform the following exercise by referring to `Chapter 4/exercises/chars_string.rs`:

- Try out whether you can get the first or the fifth character of a string by using `[0]` or `[4]`
- Compare the `bytes()` method with `chars()` on the `let greeting = "Hello, 世界!";` string

Tuples

If you want to combine a certain number of values of different types, then you can collect them in a tuple, which is enclosed between parentheses (`( )`) and separated by commas, as follows:

```
// from Chapter 4/code/tuples.rs
let thor = ("Thor", true, 3500u32);
println!("{:?}", thor); // ("Thor", true, 3500)
```

The type of `thor` is `(&str, bool, u32)`, that is: the tuple of the item's types. To extract an item on an index, use a dot-syntax:

```
println!("{} - {} - {}", thor.0, thor.1, thor.2);
```

Another way to extract items to other variables is by *destructuring* the tuple:

```
let (name, _, power) = thor;
println!("{} has {} points of power", name, power);
```

Which prints out: `Thor has 3500 points of power`.

Here the `let` statement matches the pattern on the left with the right-hand side. The `_` indicates that we are not interested in the second item of `thor`.

Tuples can only be assigned to one another or compared with each other if they are of the same type. A one-element tuple needs to be written: `let one = (1,);`.

A function that needs to return some values of different types can collect them in a tuple and return that tuple as follows:

```
fn increase_power(name: &str, power: u32) -> (&str, u32) {
  if power > 1000 {
    return (name, power * 3);
  } else {
    return (name, power * 2);
  }
}
```

If we call this with the following code snippet:

```
let (god, strength) = increase_power(thor.0, thor.2);
println!("This god {} has now {} strength", god, strength);
```

The output is: `This god Thor has now 10500 strength.`

Perform the following exercise by referring to the code at `Chapter 4/exercises/tuples_ex.rs`):

- Try to compare the tuples (2, 'a') and (5, false) and explain the error message.
- Make an empty tuple. Haven't we encountered this before? So, the unit value is in fact an empty tuple!

Structs

Often, you might need to keep several values of possibly different types together in your program; for example, the scores of the players. Let us assume that the score contains numbers that indicate the health of the players and the level at which they are playing. The first thing that you can then do to clarify your code is to give these tuples a common name, such as struct Score or better still, you can indicate the types of the values: `struct Score(i32, u8)` and we can make a score as follows:

```
let score1 = Score(73, 2);
```

These are called tuple structs because they resemble tuples very much. The values contained in them can be extracted as follows:

```
// from Chapter 4/code/structs.rs
let Score(h, l) = score1; // destructure the tuple
println!("Health {} - Level {}", h, l);
```

Which prints out: `Health 73 - Level 2.`

A tuple struct with only one field (called a newtype) gives us the possibility to create a new type that is based on an old one so that both have the same memory representation. Here is an example:

```
struct Kilograms(u32);
let weight = Kilograms(250);
let Kilograms(kgm) = weight; // extracting kgm
println!("weight is {} kilograms", kgm);
```

This prints: `weight is 250 kilograms.`

However, we will still have to remember what these numbers mean and to which players they belong. We can make coding much simpler by defining a struct with named fields:

```
struct Player {
    nname: &'static str, // nickname
    health: i32,
    level: u8
}
```

This could be defined inside `main()` or outside it, although the latter is preferred. Now, we can make player instances or objects as follows:

```
let mut pl1 = Player{ nname: "Dzenan", health: 73, level: 2 };
```

Note the curly braces (`{ }`) around the object and the `key: value` syntax. The `nname` field is a constant string, and Rust requires that we indicate its lifetime, how long this string will be needed in the program. We used the global scope, `&'static`, from the *Global constants* section in *Chapter 2, Using Variables and Types.*

We can access the fields of the instance with the dot-notation:

```
println!("Player {} is at level {}", pl1.nname, pl1.level);
```

The struct variable has to be declared as mutable if the field values can change; for example, when the player enters a new level:

```
pl1.level = 3;
```

By convention, the name of a struct always starts with a capital letter and follows CamelCase. It also defines a type of its own, which is composed of the types of its items.

Like tuples, structs can also be destructured in a `let` binding, for example:

```
let Player{ health: ht, nname: nn, .. } = pl1;
println!("Player {} has health {}", nn, ht);
```

Which prints out: `Player Dzenan has health 73`. This shows that you can rename fields, reorder them if you want, or leave fields out with.

Pointers carry out automatic dereferencing when accessing data structure elements, as follows:

```
let ps = &Player{ nname: "John", health: 95, level: 1 };
println!("{} == {}", ps.nname, (*ps).nname);
```

Structs are quite similar to the records or structs in C or even classes in other languages. In *Chapter 5, Generalizing Code with Higher-order Functions and Parametrization*, we will see how we can define methods on structs.

Perform the following exercise by referring to the code in `Chapter 4/exercises/monster.rs`:

- Define a `Monster` struct with the health and damage fields. Then, make a `Monster` and show its condition.

Enums

If something can be only one of a limited number of named values, then define it as an enum. For example, if our game needs the compass directions, we could define it as follows:

```
// from Chapter 4/code/enums.rs
enum Compass {
  North, South, East, West
}
```

And then use it as shown in `main()` or another function:

```
let direction = Compass::West;
```

The enum's values can also be of other types or structs, as in this example:

```
type species = &'static str;

enum PlanetaryMonster {
  VenusMonster(species, i32),
  MarsMonster(species, i32)
}
let martian = PlanetaryMonster::MarsMonster("Chela", 42);
```

Enums are sometimes called union types or algebraic data types in other languages. If we make a use function at the start of the code file:

```
use PlanetaryMonster::MarsMonster;
```

Then, the type can be shortened, as follows:

```
let martian = MarsMonster("Chela", 42);
```

Enums are really nice to bring clarity in your code, and they are used a lot in Rust. To apply them usefully in code, see the *Matching patterns* section of this chapter.

Result and Option

Here, we look at two kinds of enums that are pervasive in a Rust code. A *Result* is a special kind of enum that is defined in the standard library. It is used whenever something is executed, that can either end:

- Successfully, then an Ok value (of a certain type T) is returned
- With an error, then an Err value (of type E) is returned

Since this situation is so common, provision is made so that the value T and error E types can be as general or generic as possible. The Result enum is defined as follows:

```
enum Result<T, E> {
    Ok(T),
    Err(E)
}
```

An *Option* is another enum that is defined in the standard library. It is used whenever there is a value, but there can also be a possibility that there is no value. For example, suppose our program expects to read a value from the console. However, when it is run as a background program by accident, it will never get an input value. Rust wants to be on the safe side whenever it is possible, so in this case, it is better to read the value as an Option enum with two possibilities:

- Some, if there is a value
- None, if there is no value

This value can be of any type T, so option again is defined as a generic type:

```
enum Option<T> {
    Some(T),
    None
}
```

Getting input from the console

Suppose we want to capture the nicknames of our players before starting the game; how would we do that? Input/output functionality is handled by the io module in the std crate. It has a stdin() function to read input from the console. This function returns an object of the Stdin type, which is a reference to the input stream. Stdin has a read_line(buf) method to read a full line of input that ends with a new line character (when the user hits *Enter*). This input is read into a String buffer, buf. A method is a name for a function that is defined for a certain type, and it is called using dot notation, such as object.method (see *Chapter 5, Generalizing Code with Higher-order Functions and Parametrization*).

So, our code will look as follows:

```
let mut buf = String::new();
io::stdin().read_line(&mut buf);
```

However, this is not good enough for Rust; it gives us the warning, unused result which must be used. Rust is foremost a safe language and we must be ready to cope with everything than can occur. Reading a line might work and supply the input value, but it can also fail; for example, if this code was running in the background on a machine so that no console was available to get input from.

How will you cope with this? Well, read_line() returns a Result value, which can either be a real value (an Ok) when everything works fine or an error value (an Err) when there is a problem. To cope with a possible error, we need an ok() function and an expect() function; ok() converts the Result into an Option value (which contains how many bytes were read) and expect() gives this value or shows its message when an error occurs. In Rust, a program panics when an error occurs that cannot be recovered from, and the string argument from expect() is displayed to tell us where it occurred.

This is written in Rust in a chained form (and is a bit unusual the first time you see it) as follows:

```
io::stdin().read_line(&mut buf).ok().expect("Error!");
```

Rust allows us to write these successive calls on separate lines, which clarifies the code a lot for most people:

```
    // from Chapter 4/code/input.rs
use std::io;

fn main() {
  println!("What's your name, noble warrior?");
  let mut buf = String::new();
```

```
    io::stdin().read_line(&mut buf)
        .ok()
        .expect("Failed to read line");
    println!("{}, that's a mighty name indeed!", buf);
}
```

When we run this code from the command line, we get the following conversation:

What's your name, noble warrior?

Riddick

Riddick

, that's a mighty name indeed!

Can you guess why that's a mighty name indeed! appears on a new line? This is because the input buf still contains a newline character, \n! Luckily, we have a trim() method to remove trailing and leading whitespace from a string. If we insert the line shown in the following snippet:

```
let name = buf.trim();
println!("{}, that's a mighty name indeed!", name);
```

We now get a correct output: Riddick, that's a mighty name indeed!

In case the input does not succeed, our program will crash with the following output:

```
What's your name, noble warrior?
thread '<main>' panicked at 'Failed to read line
```

How would we read in a positive integer number from the console?

```
// from Chapter 4/code/pattern_match.rs
let mut buf = String::new();
io::stdin().read_line(&mut buf)
    .ok()
    .expect("Failed to read number");
let input_num: Result<u32, _> = buf.trim().parse();
```

We read the number in from the console in a buf String buffer and trim() the value; expect() will show us the message if something goes wrong. However, what we have read in is still a String, so we must convert the String to a number.

The parse() method tries to convert the input to an unsigned 32-bit integer in this case. What it returns is in fact a Result value again; this can either be an integer (Ok<u32>) or an error (Err) when the conversion fails.

We will encounter more examples of Option and Result in the *Generics* section of *Chapter 5, Generalizing Code with Higher-order Functions and Parametrization*.

Matching patterns

But how will we test whether `input_num` from the previous section, which is of the Result type, contains a value or not? When the value is an `Ok(T)` function, the `unwrap()` function can extract `T` like this:

```
println!("Unwrap found {}", input_num.unwrap());
```

Which prints: `Unwrap found 42`. However, when the result is an `Err` value, this lets the program crash with a panic, which is `thread '<main>' panicked at 'called 'Result::unwrap()' on an 'Err' value'`. This is bad!

To solve this, no complex if – else constructs will be enough; we need Rust's magical match here, which has a lot more possibilities than the switch in other languages, and is used frequently when handling errors:

```
match input_num {
    Ok(num) => println!("{}", num),
    Err(ex) => println!("Please input an integer number! {}", ex)
};
```

The `match` function tests the value of an expression against all possible values. Only the code (which can be a block) after the `=>` of the first matching branch is executed. All branches are separated by commas. In this case, the same number that is given as input is printed out. There is no fall through from one branch to the next, so a break statement is not necessary; this enables us to avoid a common bug in C++.

In order to continue working with the return value of `match`, we have to bind that value to a variable, which is possible because match itself is an expression:

```
let num = match input_num {
        Ok(num) => num,
        Err(_)  => 0
};
```

This `match` extracts the number from `input_num` so that we can compare it with other numbers or calculate with it. Both branches must return a value of the same type; this is why we returned 0 in the `Err` case (supposing we expect a number greater than 0).

An alternative way to get the Result or Option value is by using the `if let` construct as follows:

```
if let Ok(val) = input_num {
    println!("Matched {:?}!", val);
} else {
    println!("No match!");
}
```

The `input_num` function is destructured and if it contains a value `val`, this is extracted. In certain cases, this can simplify the code, but you lose the exhaustive match check. The same principle can be applied inside a `while` loop as follows:

```
while let Ok(val) = input_num {
    println!("Matched {:?}!", val);
    if val == 42 { break }
}
```

With `match`, all possible values must be covered, which is the case if we match with a Result, Option (Some or None is pretty exhaustive), or some other enum value.

However, look what happens when we test on a string slice for example:

```
// from Chapter 4/code/pattern_match2.rs
let magician = "Gandalf";
match magician {
    "Gandalf" => println!("A good magician!"),
    "Sauron"  => println!("A magician turned bad!")
}
```

This `match` on `magician` gives us an error: non-exhaustive patterns: _ not covered. After all, there are other magicians besides "Gandalf" and "Sauron"! The compiler even gives us the solution: use an underscore (_) for all other possibilities; so, this is a complete match:

```
match magician {
    "Gandalf" => println!("A good magician!"),
    "Sauron"  => println!("A magician turned bad!"),
    _         => println!("No magician turned up!")
}
```

 To be always on the safe side, use match when testing on the possible values of a variable or expression!

The left-hand side of a branch can contain several values if they are separated by a | sign or an inclusive range of values written as start ... end. The following code snippet shows this in action:

```
let magical_number: i32 = 42;
match magical_number {
    // Match a single value
    1 => println!("Unity!"),
    // Match several values
    2 | 3 | 5 | 7 | 11 => println!("Ok, these are primes"),
```

```
    // Match an inclusive range
    40...42 => println!("It is contained in this range"),
    // Handle the rest of cases
    _ => println!("No magic at all!"),
}
```

This prints out: It is contained in this range. The matched value can be captured in a variable (here num) using the @ symbol as follows:

```
num @ 40...42 => println!("{} is contained in this range", num)
```

Which prints: 42 is contained in this range.

Matches are even more powerful than this; the expression that is being matched can be destructured on the left-hand side, and this can even be combined with the if conditions that are called *guards*:

```
let loki = ("Loki", true, 800u32);
    match loki {
        (name, demi, _) if demi => {
                    print!("This is a demigod ");
                    println!("called {}", name);
                },
        (name, _, _) if name == "Thor" =>
                    println!("This is Thor!"),
        (_, _, pow) if pow <= 1000 =>
                    println!("This is a powerless god"),
        _ => println!("This is something else")
    }
```

Which prints out: This is a demigod called Loki.

Note that since demi is a Boolean, we don't have to write if demi == true. If you want to do nothing in a branch, then write => {}. Destructuring works not only for tuples, like this example, but it can also be applied for structs.

Perform the following exercise:

What happens if you move the _ branch from the last position upwards? See an example in Chapter 4/exercises/pattern_match.rs.

The use of the .. and ... notations can be confusing, so here is a summary of the situations in Rust 1.0:

	What works	Does not work
for in	.. exclusive	. . .
Match	... inclusive	..

Summary

In this chapter, we increased our capabilities for working with composite data in Rust, from strings, arrays and vectors, and slices of both, to tuples, structs, and enums. We also discovered that pattern matching, combined with destructuring and guards, is a very powerful tool for writing clear and elegant code.

In the following chapter, we will see that functions are much more powerful than we expected. Furthermore, we will discover that structs can have methods by implementing traits, almost like classes and interfaces in other languages.

5

Generalizing Code with Higher-order Functions and Parametrization

Now that we have the data structures and control constructs in place, we can start to discover the functional and object-oriented features of Rust, which make it a really expressive language. We will cover the following topics in this chapter:

- Higher-order functions and closures
- Iterators
- Consumers and adapters
- Generic data structures and functions
- Error handling
- Methods on structs
- Traits
- Using trait constraints
- Built-in traits and operator overloading

Higher-order functions and closures

By now, we know how to use functions, as shown in the following example where the triples function changes our strength, but only if the return value of triples is assigned to strength:

```
// see code in Chapter 5/code/higher_functions.rs
let mut strength = 26;
println!("My tripled strength equals {}",triples(strength)); // 78
```

```
println!("My strength is still {}", strength); // 26
strength = triples(strength);
println!("My strength is now {}", strength); // 78
```

With `triples` defined as `fn triples(s: i32) -> i32 { 3 * s }`, s represents strength.

Suppose our player smashes an amazing power stone so that his strength is tripled and the resulting strength is tripled again, so we could write `triples(triples(s))`. We can also write a function to do this, but it would be even more general to have a function, let's call it again, that could apply a certain function f, of the F type upon its result, enabling us to create all kinds of new game tricks, as follows:

```
fn again (f: F, s: i32) -> i32  { f(f(s)) }
```

However, this is not enough information for Rust; the compiler will ask us to explain what the F type is. We can make this clear by adding `<F: Fn(i32) -> i32>` before the parameter list:

```
fn again<F: Fn(i32) -> i32>(f: F , s: i32) -> i32 {
    f(f(s))
}
```

The expression between `<` `>` (angle brackets) tells us that F is a function, Fn ,that takes `i32` as a parameter and returns an `i32` function.

Now look at the definition of triples. that's exactly what this function does (triples has the signature of type F), so we can call again with triples as the first parameter:

```
strength = again(triples, strength);
println!("I got so lucky to turn my strength into {}", strength); //
702 (= 3 * 3 * 78)
```

The `again` function is a *higher-order function*, which means that it is a function that takes another function (or more than one function) as a parameter.

Often, simple functions such as `triples` are not even defined as a named function:

```
strength = 78;
let triples = |n| { 3 * n };
strength = again(triples, strength);
println!("My strength is now {}", strength); // 702
```

Here, we have an *anonymous function* or *closure*, |n| { 3 * n }, that takes an n
parameter and returns its tripled value. The || (vertical bars) mark the start of
a closure, and they contain the parameters that are passed to it (when there are
no parameters, it is written as ||). There is no need to indicate the type of the
parameters or the return value as a closure can infer their types from the context
in which it is called.

The triples function is only a binding to a name so that we can refer to the closure
in another code. We can even leave that name out and put the closure inline,
as follows:

```
strength = 78;
strength = again(|n| { 3 * n }, strength);
println!("My strength is now {}", strength); // 702
```

The closure is called with the n parameter that takes the value of s, which is a copy of
strength. The braces can also be left out to simplify the closure as follows:

```
strength = again(|n| 3 * n , strength);
```

So, why is it called a closure? This becomes more apparent in the following example:

```
let x: i32 = 42;
let print_add = |s| {
    println!("x is {}", x);
    x + s
};
let res = print_add(strength);
// here the closure is called and "x is 42" is printed
assert_eq!(res, 744); // 42 + 702
```

The print_add() closure has one argument and returns a 32-bit integer. The
print_add closure knows the value of x and all other variables that are available in
its surrounding scope—it *closes* them in. A closure with no arguments has the empty
parameter list, ||.

There is also a special kind of closure called a moving closure, which is indicated by
the move keyword. A normal closure only needs a reference to the variables that it
encloses, but a moving closure takes ownership of all the enclosing variables.

The preceding example would be written with a moving closure as follows:

```
let m: i32 = 42;
let print_add_move = move |s| {
    println!("m is {}", m);
    m + s
};
let res = print_add_move(strength); // strength == 702
assert_eq!(res, 744); // 42 + 702
```

Moving closures are mostly used when a program works with different concurrent threads (You can see this in *Chapter 8, Concurrency and Parallelism*).

As you will see in the following sections, higher-order functions and closures are used throughout Rust because they can make code much more concise and readable, and they are useful to generalize a computation.

Iterators

An Iterator is an object that returns the items of a collection in sequence, from the first item to the last one. To return the following item, it uses a next() method. Here, we have an opportunity to use Option: because an iterator can have no more values at a certain next() call, next() returns Option: a Some(value) when there is a value, and None when there are no more values.

The simplest object that has this behavior is a range of numbers, 0...n. Every time we used a for loop, such as for i in 0...n, the underlying iterator mechanism was put to work. Let's see an example:

```
// see code in Chapter 5/code/iterators.rs
let mut rng = 0..7;
println!("> {:?}", rng.next()); // prints Some(0)
println!("> {:?}", rng.next()); // prints Some(1)
for n in rng {
    print!("{} - ", n);
} // prints 2 - 3 - 4 - 5 - 6 -
```

Here, we see next() at work, which produces 0, 1, and so on; the for loop continues until the end.

Perform the following exercise:

In the previous example, we saw that `next()` returns a `Some` object, a variant of the `Option` type (see the *Result and Option* section of *Chapter 4, Structuring Data and Matching Patterns*). Write an endless loop over `rng` with `next()` and see what happens. How would you break the endless loop? Use a match on the `Option` value. (for an example, see `Chapter 5/exercises/range_next.rs`). In fact, the `for` loop that we saw right before this exercise is syntactic sugar for this `loop` – `match` construct.

Iterators are also the preferred way to loop over arrays or slices. Let's revisit the aliens array, `let aliens = ["Cherfer", "Fynock", "Shirack", "Zuxu"];",` from *Chapter 4, Structuring Data and Matching Patterns*. Instead of using the index to show all the items one by one, let's do it the iterator way with the `iter()` function:

```
for alien in aliens.iter() {
  print!("{} / ", alien)
  // process alien
}
```

Which prints out: `Cherfer / Fynock / Shirack / Zuxu /`. The alien variable is of the `&str` type, which is a reference to each of the items in turn. (Technically, it is of the `&&str` type here because the items themselves are of the `&str` type, but this is not relevant to the point being made here.) This is much more performant and safe because Rust doesn't have to do index-bounds checking, we're always certain to move within the memory of the array.

An even shorter way is to write:

```
for alien in &aliens {
  print!("{} / ", alien)
}
```

An alien array is also of the `&str` type, but the `print!` macro automatically dereferences this. If you want them to print out in the reverse order, do `aliens.iter().rev()`. The other iterators that we encountered in the previous chapter were the `chars()` and `split()` methods on `Strings`.

Iterators are lazy by nature; they do not generate values unless asked, and we ask them by calling the `next()` method or applying `for` in the loop. This makes sense as we don't want to allocate one million integers in the following binding:

```
let rng = 0..1000_000; // _ makes the number 1000000 more readable
```

We want to allocate memory only when we need it.

Consumers and adapters

Now, we will see some examples that show why iterators are so useful. Iterators are lazy and have to be activated by invoking a *consumer* to start using the values. Let's start with a range of the numbers from 0 to 999. To make this into a vector, we apply the `collect()` consumer:

```
// see code in Chapter 5/code/adapters_consumers.rs
let rng = 0..1000;
let rngvec = rng.collect::<Vec<i32>>();
println!("{:?}", rngvec);
```

Which prints out the range (we shortened the output with ...): [0, 1, 2, 3, 4, ... , 999]

The `collect()` loops through the entire iterator and collects all of the elements into a container, here in the `Vec<i32>` type. That container does not have to be an iterator. Notice that we indicate the item type of the vector with `Vec<i32>`, but we could have also written it as `Vec<_>`. The `collect::<Vec<i32>>()` notation is new; it indicates that collect is a parametrized method that can work with generic types, as you will see in the next section. That line could also have been written as:

```
let rngvec: Vec<i32> = rng.collect();
```

The `find()` consumer gets the first value of the iterator that makes its condition (here, `>= 42`) true and returns it as an `Option` function, for example:

```
let forty_two = rng.find(|n| *n >= 42);
println!("{:?}", forty_two);  // prints out Some(42)
```

The value of `find` is an `Option` function because the condition could be false for all items and then it would return a `None` value. The condition is wrapped in a `|n| *n >= 42` closure, which is applied on every item of the iterator through an n reference; this is why we have to dereference `*n` to get the value.

Suppose we only want even numbers in our range, producing a new range by testing a closure condition on each item. This can be done with the `filter()` function, which is an adapter because it produces a new iterator from the old one. Its result can be collected just like any iterator:

```
let rng_even = rng.filter(|n| is_even(*n))
                .collect::<Vec<i32>>();
println!("{:?}", rng_even);
```

Here, `is_even` is the following function:

```
fn is_even(n: i32) -> bool {
  n % 2 == 0
}
```

This prints out: [0, 2, 4, ..., 996, 998] showing that odd integers are filtered out.

Notice how we can chain our consumers/adapters by just applying collect() on the result of filter() with .collect().

Now, what would we do if we wanted to cube (n * n * n) with every item in the resulting iterator? We can produce a new range by applying a closure to each item in it with the map() function:

```
let rng_even_pow3 = rng.filter(|n| is_even(*n))
                       .map(|n| n * n * n)
                       .collect::<Vec<i32>>();
println!("{:?}", rng_even_pow3);
```

Which now prints out: [0, 8, 64, ..., 988047936, 994011992].

If you only want the first five results, insert a take(5) adapter before the collect function. The resulting vector will then contain [0, 8, 64, 216, 512].

So, if you see the warning, unused result which must be used: iterator adaptors are lazy and do nothing unless consumed message while compiling, you know what to do—call a consumer!

To see all the consumers and adapters, consult the documentation of the std::iter module.

Perform the following exercise:

Another very powerful consumer is the fold() function. The following example calculates the sum of the first hundred integers. It starts with a base value 0, which is also the initial value of the sum accumulator, and then iterates and adds every n item to sum:

```
let sum = (0..101).fold(0, |sum, n| sum + n);
println!("{}", sum); // prints out 5050
```

Now, calculate the product of all the cubes of the integers in the range from 1 to 6. The result should be 1,728,000, but look out for the base value! As the second exercise, subtract all the items from the [1, 9, 2, 3, 14, 12] array, starting from 0 (that is, 0, 1, 9, 2, and so on). This should result in 41. (As a hint, remember that an iterator item is a reference; for some example code, refer to Chapter 5/exercises/fold.rs).

Generic data structures and functions

Genericity is the capacity to write code once, without or partly specified types, so that the code can be used for many different types. Rust has this capacity in abundance and applies it for both data structures and functions.

A composite data structure is generic if the type of its items can be of a general <T> type. T can be an i32, an f64, a String, or a struct type such as Person that we coded ourselves. So, we can have not only Vec<f64> but also Vec<Person>. If you make T a concrete type, then you must substitute T with that type everywhere T appears in the definition of the data structure.

Our data structure can be parametrized with a generic <T> type, so it has multiple concrete definitions — it is polymorphic. Rust makes extensive use of this concept, which we already encountered in *Chapter 4, Structuring Data and Matching Patterns* when we talked about arrays, vectors, slices, and the Result and Option types.

Suppose you want to define a struct with two fields, first and second, but you want to keep the type of these fields generic. We can define this as follows:

```
// see code in Chapter 5/code/generics.rs
struct Pair<T> {
    first: T,
    second: T,
}
```

We can now define a pair of magic numbers, or a pair of magicians, or whatever we want, as follows:

```
let magic_pair: Pair<u32> = Pair { first: 7, second: 42 };
let pair_of_magicians: Pair<&str> = Pair { first: "Gandalf", second:
"Sauron" };
```

What if we wanted to write functions that work with generic data structures? They would also have to be generic, right? As a simple example, how would we write a function that returns the second item of a pair? We can do it as follows:

```
fn second<T>(pair: Pair<T>) {
  pair.second;
}
```

We could call it as let a = second(magic_pair); producing 42.

Note the <T> character right after the function name; this is how generic functions are declared.

Let's now investigate why `Option` and `Result` are so powerful. Here is the definition of the `Option` type again:

```
enum Option<T> {
    Some(T),
    None
}
```

From this, we can define multiple concrete types as follows:

```
let x: Option<i8> = Some(5);
let pi: Option<f64> = Some(3.14159265359);
let none: Option<f64> = None;
let none2 = None::<f64>;
let name: Option<&str> = Some("Joyce");
```

When the type does not correspond with the value, a mismatched types error occurs, similar to that in `let magic: Option<f32> = Some(42)`.

We can define a `Person` struct as follows:

```
struct Person {
    name: &'static str,
    id:   i32
}
```

We can also define a few `Person` objects as follows:

```
let p1 = Person{ name: "James Bond", id: 7 };
let p2 = Person{ name: "Vin Diesel", id: 12 };
let p3 = Person{ name: "Robin Hood", id: 42 };
```

Then, using these, we can make `Option` or a vector for `Person`:

```
let op1: Option<Person> = Some(p1);
let pvec: Vec<Person> = vec![p2, p3];
```

You should use the `Option` type in a situation where you expect to get a value, but there is a possibility that no value will be given. A typical scenario would be user input.

Somewhat related is the `Result` type that we first encountered in the *Result and Option* section of *Chapter 4, Structuring Data and Matching Patterns*. This is used when a computation should return a result, but it can also return an error if something goes wrong. Result is defined with two generic types — T and E — as follows:

```
enum Result<T, E> {
    Ok(T),
    Err(E)
}
```

It again shows Rust's commitment to be on the safe side; if it's `Ok`, it will give back a value of the `T` type, if there is a problem, then it will give back the error that will be a value of the `E` type (which is usually an error message string). So, we could read them also as `Ok(what)` and `Err(why)`, where `what` has the `T` type and `why` has the `E` type.

So, why are Option and Result killer features of Rust? Remember from *Chapter 4, Structuring Data and Matching Patterns* in the section *Result and Option* how we used `Option` when getting a number input? Here, it is given again:

```
let input_num: Result<u32, _> = buf.trim().parse();
```

In other languages such as Java or C#, parsing the input to a number could result in an exception (when the input contains non-numeric characters or when it has nothing or null), and you would have to use a resource heavy `try/catch` to construct to deal with it.

In Rust, the result of `parse()` is a Result, and we just test the `Result` return value with a `match`, which is a much simpler mechanism:

```
match input_num {
    Ok(num)  => println!("{}", num),
    Err(ex) => println!("Please input an integer number! {}", ex)
};
```

Here is another example of how we can use `Result` to return an error condition. We calculate the square root of a floating point number with the `std::num::Float::sqrt()` function:

```
fn sqroot(r: f32) -> Result<f32, String> {
  if r < 0.0 {
    return Err("Number cannot be negative!".to_string());
  }
  Ok(Float::sqrt(r))
}
```

We guard against taking the square root of a negative number (which would give NaN short for Not a Number) by returning an `Err` value.

```
let m = sqroot(42.0);
```

This prints out: `The square root of 42 is 6.480741.`

In the calling code, we use our trusted pattern match mechanism to distinguish between the two cases:

```
match m {
    Ok(sq) => println!("The square root of 42 is {}", sq),
    Err(str) => println!("{}", str)
}
```

With `let m = sqroot(-5.0);`, the error message is printed as `Number cannot be negative!`.

> The use of match for both `Option` and `Result` values ensures that no null values or errors can propagate through your code, which leaves no room for null pointer runtime errors or other exceptions to crash your program.

Error handling

A Rust program must be maximally prepared to handle unforeseen errors, but unexpected things can always happen, such as the division of an integer by zero:

```
// see code in Chapter 5/code/errors.rs
let x = 3;
let y = 0;
x / y;
```

When this happens, the program stops with the following message: `thread '<main>' panicked at 'attempted to divide by zero'.`

Panics

A situation could occur that is so bad (like when dividing by zero) that it is no longer useful to continue running the program, that is, we cannot recover from the error. In this case, we can invoke the `panic!("message")` macro, which will release all the resources owned by the thread, report the message, and then make the program exit. We could improve the previous code as follows:

```
if (y == 0) { panic!("Division by 0 occurred, exiting"); }
println!("{}", div(x, y));
```

Here, `div` is the following function:

```
fn div(x: i32, y: i32) -> f32 {
    (x / y) as f32
}
```

A number of other macros such as the `assert!` family can also be used to signal such unwanted conditions:

```
assert!(x == 5); //thread <main> panicked at assertion failed: x == 5
assert!( x == 5, "x is not equal to 5!");
// thread <main> panicked at "x is not equal to 5!"
assert_eq!(x, 5); // thread '<main>' panicked at 'assertion failed:
(left: `3`, right: `5`)',
```

When the condition is not true, they result in a panic situation and exit. The error message that is given as the second parameter of `assert!` will be printed out if it is present, otherwise the general message, `assertion failed`, will be given. The `assert!` function is mostly useful to test for pre- and post-conditions.

Portions of code that would not be normally executed can contain the `unreachable!` macro, which will panic when it is executed:

```
unreachable!();
// thread '<main>' panicked at 'internal error: entered unreachable
code'
```

Failures

In most cases, we would like to attempt to recover from the error and let the program continue. Fortunately, we have already seen the basic handling techniques to do just this in the *Result and Option* section of *Chapter 4, Structuring Data and Matching Patterns* and the *Generic data structures and functions* section of this chapter.

The `Option<T>` enum can be used when we expect a value; at this point, a `Some(T)` enum is given and a `None` value is returned when there was no value or in case of failure. In this way, Rust forces *nothingness* to appear in a clear and syntactically identifiable form, leaving no room for null pointer runtime errors.

The `Result<T, E>` enum can be used to return an `Ok(T)` value in the normal (success) case and an `Err(E)` value in the failure case, containing information about the error. In the examples in the previous section, we used Result to safely read a value from the keyboard and make a safe function to calculate the square root of a number.

Methods on structs

Now, we'll see how Rust caters for more object-oriented developers who are used to the `object.method()` type of notation instead of `function(object)`. In Rust, we can define *methods* on a struct, which pretty much compares to the traditional `class` concept.

Suppose we are building a game in which the action takes place on a planet in a distant solar system that is inhabited by hostile aliens. For this game, let's define an `Alien` struct as follows:

```
// see code in Chapter 5/code/methods.rs
struct Alien {
    health: u32,
    damage: u32
}
```

Here, `health` is the alien's condition, and `damage` is the amount your health is decreased when it attacks. We can make an alien as follows:

```
let mut bork = Alien{ health: 100, damage: 5 };
```

The `health` parameter cannot be more than `100`, but we cannot impose this constraint when we make a struct instance. The solution is to define a `new` method for aliens where we can test the value:

```
impl Alien {
    fn new(mut h: u32, d: u32) -> Alien {
        // constraints:
        if h > 100 { h = 100; }
        Alien { health: h, damage: d }
    }
}
```

We can then construct a new `Alien` array as follows:

```
let mut berserk = Alien::new(150, 15);
```

We define the `new` method (and all other methods) inside an `impl Alien` block, which is separate from the `Alien` struct definition. It returns an `Alien` object after all constraints have been applied. We call it on the `Alien` struct itself as `Alien::new()`. Since it is a *static method*, we don't call it on an `Alien` instance. Such a new method closely resembles a constructor from object-oriented languages. The fact that it is called `new` is merely by convention since we could have called it `create()` or `give_birth()`. Another static method could be a warning that is given by all aliens:

```
fn warn() -> &'static str {
    "Leave this planet immediately or perish!"
}
```

This can be called as follows:

```
println!("{}", Alien::warn());
```

When a specific alien attacks, we can define a method for that alien as follows:

```
fn attack(&self) {
    println!("I attack! Your health lowers with {} damage points.",
    self.damage);
}
```

And call it on the alien `berserk` as follows: `berserk.attack();`. A reference to `berserk` (the `Alien` object on which the method is invoked) is passed as `&self` to the method. In fact, `self` is similar to the `self` in Python or this in Java or C#. An instance method always has `&self` as parameter, in contrast to a static method.

Here, the object is passed immutably, but what if attacking you also lowers the alien's own health? Let's add a second attack method:

```
fn attack(&self) {
    self.health -= 10;
}
```

However, Rust rejects this with two compiler errors. First, it says, `cannot assign to immutable field self.health`. We can remedy this by passing a mutable reference to `self` like this: `fn attack(&mut self)`. But now Rust complains, `duplicate definition of value 'attack'`. This means that Rust does not allow two methods with the same name; there is no method overloading in Rust. This is because of the way type inference works.

By changing the name to `attack_and_suffer`, we get this:

```
fn attack_and_suffer(&mut self, damage_from_other: u32) {
  self.health -= damage_from_other;
}
```

After calling `berserk.attack_and_suffer(31);`, berserk's health is now 69 (where 31 is the number of damage points inflicted upon berserk by another attacking alien).

No method overloading means that we can only define one new function (which is optional anyway). We could invent different names for our constructors, which is good from the point of view of code documentation. Otherwise, you could go for what is called the `Builder` pattern on which you can find more information at `http://doc.rust-lang.org/book/method-syntax.html#builder-pattern`.

 Note that, in Rust, methods can also be defined on tuples and enums.

Perform the following exercise:

Complex numbers such as 2 + 5i (i is the square root of -1) have a real part (here 2) and an imaginary part (5); both are floating point numbers. Define a `Complex` struct and some methods for it:

- A `new` method to construct a complex number.

- A `to_string` method that prints a complex number such as 2 + 5i or 2 - 5i (As a hint, use the `format!` macro that works in the same way as `println!` but returns a `String`.)

- An `add` method to add two complex numbers; this is a new complex number where the real part is the sum of the real parts of the operands and the same is applicable for the imaginary part as well.

- A `times_ten` method that changes the object itself by multiplying both parts by 10 (As a hint, think carefully about the method's argument.)

- As a bonus, make an `abs` method that calculates the absolute value of a complex number. (go to `http://en.wikipedia.org/wiki/Absolute_value`.)

Now, test your methods! (for an example code, refer to `Chapter 5/exercises/complex.rs`.) Rust defines a `Complex` type in crate `num`.

Traits

What if our game is really diversely populated? That is, besides aliens, we also have zombies and predators and, needless to say, they all want to attack. Can we abstract their common behavior into something they all share? Of course, in Rust, we say that they have a trait in common, which is analogous to an interface or a super class in other languages. Let's call this trait Monster and because they all want to attack, the first version could be as follows:

```
// see code in Chapter 5/code/traits.rs
trait Monster {
    fn attack(&self);
}
```

A trait only contains a description of methods, that is, their type declarations or signatures, but it has no real implementation. This is logical because zombies, predators, and aliens could each have their own method of attack. So, there is no body of code between { } after the function signature, but don't forget the ; to close it off.

When we want to implement the Monster trait for the Alien struct, we write the following code:

```
impl Monster for Alien {

}
```

When we compile this, Rust throws the not all trait items implemented, missing: 'attack' error. This is nice because Rust reminds us which methods from a trait we have forgotten to implement. The following code would make it pass:

```
impl Monster for Alien {
  fn attack(&self) {
    println!("I attack! Your health lowers with {} damage points.",
self.damage);
  }
}
```

So, the trait implementation for a type must provide the real code, which will be executed when that method is called on an Alien object. If a Zombie attack is twice as bad, its Monster implementation could be as follows:

```
impl Monster for Zombies {
  fn attack(&self) {
    println!("I bite you! Your health lowers with {} damage points.",
    2 * self.damage);
  }
}
```

We could add other methods to our trait, such as a new method, a `noise` method, and an `attack_with_sound` method:

```
trait Monster {
    fn new(hlt: u32, dam: u32) -> Self;
    fn attack(&self);
    fn noise(&self) -> &'static str;
    fn attacks_with_sound(&self) {
      println!("The Monster attacks by making an awkward sound {}",
      self.noise());
    }
}
```

Note that in the `new` method, the resulting object is of the `Self` type, which becomes the `Alien` or `Zombie` implementer type in a real implementation of the trait.

The functions that appear in a trait are called methods. Methods differ from functions because they have `&self` as a parameter; this means that they have the object on which they are invoked as a parameter, for example, `fn noise(&self) -> &'static str`. When we call it with `zmb1.noise()`, the `zmb1` object becomes self.

A trait can provide default code for a method (similar to the `attack_with_sound` method here). The implementer type can choose to take this default code or override it with its own version. Code in a trait method can also call upon other methods in the trait with `self.method()`, similar to `attack_with_sound` where `self.noise()` is called.

The full implementation of the `Monster` trait for the `Zombie` type could then be as follows:

```
impl Monster for Zombie {
  fn new(mut h: u32, d: u32) -> Zombie {
    // constraints:
    if h > 100 { h = 100; }
    Zombie { health: h, damage: d }
  }
  fn attack(&self) {
    println!("The Zombie bites! Your health lowers with {} damage
    points.", 2 * self.damage);
  }
  fn noise(&self) -> &'static str {
    "Aaargh!"
  }
}
```

Here is a short fragment of our game scenario:

```
let zmb1 = Zombie { health: 75, damage: 15 };
println!("Oh no, I hear: {}", zmb1.noise());
zmb1.attack();
```

It prints out: `Oh no, I hear: Aaargh!`

`The Zombie bites! Your health lowers with 30 damage points.`

Traits are not limited to structs; they can be implemented on any type. A type can also implement many different traits. All the different implemented methods are compiled to a version that is specific for their type, so after compilation, there exists, for example, a new method for `Alien`, `Zombie`, and `Predator`.

Implementing all of the methods in a trait can be tedious work. For example, we probably want to be able to show our creatures in this way:

```
println!("{:?}", zmb1);
```

Unfortunately, this gives us `the trait 'core::fmt::Debug' is not implemented for the type 'Zombie'` compiler error. So, from the message, we can infer that this `{:?}` uses a `Debug` trait. If we look this up in the docs, we will find that we must implement an `fmt` method (specifying a way to format the object). However, the compiler once again helps us here; if we prefix our `Zombie` struct definition with the attribute `#[derive(Debug)]`, then a default code version is generated automatically:

```
#[derive(Debug)]
struct Zombie { health: u32, damage: u32 }
```

The `println!("{:?}", zmb1);` snippet now shows this: `Zombie { health: 75, damage: 15 }`.

This also works for a whole list of other traits. (see the *Built-in traits and Operator Overloading* section in this chapter and `http://rustbyexample.com/trait/derive.html`.)

Using trait constraints

Back in the *Generic data structures and functions* section, we made a `sqroot` function to calculate the square root of a 32-bit floating point number:

```
fn sqroot(r: f32) -> Result<f32, String> {
    if r < 0.0 {
        return Err("Number cannot be negative!".to_string());
```

```
    }
    Ok(f32::sqrt(r))
}
```

What if we want to calculate the square root of an f64 number? It would be very unpractical to make a different version for each type. The first attempt would be to just replace f32 with a generic type <T>:

```
// see code in Chapter 5/code/trait_constraints.rs
extern crate num;
use num::traits::Float;
fn sqroot<T>(r: T) -> Result<T, String> {
  if r < 0.0 {
    return Err("Number cannot be negative!".to_string());
  }
  Ok(num::traits::Float::sqrt(r))
}
```

However, Rust would not agree because it doesn't know anything about T, and it will give multiple errors (num is an external library which is imported with extern crate num, see *Chapter 7, Organizing Code and Macros*):

```
binary operation `<` cannot be applied to type `T`
the trait `core::marker::Copy` is not implemented for the type `T`
the trait `core::num::NumCast` is not implemented for the type `T`
...
```

All the traits that are missing are implemented by the Float trait. We can assert that T must implement this trait as fn sqroot<T: num::traits::Float>. This is called putting a trait constraint or a trait bound on the T type, and this ensures that the function can use all the methods of the specified trait.

To be as general as possible, we also use the special indicator for 0, which exists in the num::traits::Float trait and is named num::zero(); so, our function now becomes as follows:

```
fn sqroot<T: num::traits::Float>(r: T) -> Result<T, String> {
  if r < num::zero() {
    return Err("Number cannot be negative!".to_string());
  }
  Ok(num::traits::Float::sqrt(r))
}
```

This works for both the following calls:

```
println!("The square root of {} is {:?}", 42.0f32, sqroot(42.0f32) );
println!("The square root of {} is {:?}", 42.0f64, sqroot(42.0f64) );
```

This gives the output as:

```
The square root of 42 is Ok(6.480741)
The square root of 42 is Ok(6.480741)
```

However, we will get an error if we try to call `sqroot` on an integer as follows:

```
println!("The square root of {} is {:?}", 42, sqroot(42) );
```

We get an error, `the trait ‘std::num::Float‘ is not implemented for the type ‘_‘ [E0277]`, because an integer is not a `Float` type.

Our `sqroot` function is generic and works for any `Float` type. The compiler creates a different executable `sqroot` method for any type that it is supposed to work with—in this case, `f32` and `f64`. Rust applies this mechanism when a function call is polymorphic, that is, when a function can accept arguments of different type. This is called `static` dispatch and no runtime overhead is involved. This should be contrasted with how Java interfaces work where the dispatching is done dynamically at runtime by the Java Virtual Machine. However, Rust also has a form of dynamic dispatch; for more details on this, go to `http://doc.rust-lang.org/1.0.0-beta/book/static-and-dynamic-dispatch.html`.

Another way to write the same trait constraint is with a `where` clause as follows:

```
fn sqroot<T>(r: T) -> Result<T, String> where T: num::traits::Float {
    ... }
```

Why does this other form exist? Well, there can be more than one generic `T` and `U` types. In addition, each type can be constrained to multiple traits (which is indicated by a + between the traits) such as `Trait1`, `Trait2`, and so on, like in this fictitious example:

```
fn multc<T: Trait1, U: Trait1 + Trait2>(x: T, y: U) {}
```

With the `where` syntax, this can be made much more readable as follows:

```
fn multc<T, U>(x: T, y: U) where T: Trait1, U: Trait1 + Trait2 {}
```

Perform the following exercise:

Define a `Draw` trait with a `draw` method. Define the `S1` struct type with an integer field and the `S2` struct type with a float field.

Implement the `Draw` trait for `S1` and `S2` (draw prints the values and is surrounded by ***).

Make a generic `draw_object` function that takes any object that implements `Draw`.

Test these! (see the example code in `Chapter 5/exercises/draw_trait.rs`)

Built-in traits and operator overloading

The Rust standard library is packed with traits, which are used all over the place. For example, there are traits for:

- Comparing objects (the Eq and PartialEq traits).

- Ordering objects (the Ord and PartialOrd traits).

- Creating an empty object (the Default trait).

- Formatting a value using {:?} (the Debug trait, which defines a fmt method).

- Copying an object (the Clone trait).

- Adding objects (the Add trait, which defines an add method)

 The + operator is just a nice way to use; add: n + m is the same as n.add(m). So, if we implement the Add trait, we can use the + operator; this is called operator overloading. A lot of other traits can also be used to overload operators, such as Sub(-), Mul(*), Deref (*v), Index([]), and so on.

- Freeing the resources of an object when it goes out of scope (the Drop trait in other words, the object has a destructor)

In the *Iterators* section, we described how an iterator works and used it on ranges and arrays. In fact, iterator is also defined as a trait in Rust in std::iter::Iterator. From the docs for iterator (refer to http://doc.rust-lang.org/core/iter/trait.Iterator.html), we see that we only need to define the next() method, which advances the iterator to return the next value as an option. When next() is implemented for the type of your object, we can then use a for in loop to iterate over the object.

Summary

In this chapter, we learned all kinds of techniques to make our code more flexible by using higher-order functions, closures, iterators, and generic types and functions. We then reviewed the basic error-handling mechanisms that make good use of generic types.

We also discovered the object-oriented nature of Rust, by defining methods on structs and implementing traits. Finally, we saw that traits are the structuring concept of Rust.

In the next chapter, we will expose the crown jewels of the Rust language, which form the foundation of its memory safety behavior.

6
Pointers and Memory Safety

This is probably the most important chapter of this book. Here, we describe in detail the unique way in which the Rust borrow-checker mechanism detects problems at compile time to prevent memory safety errors. This is fundamental to everything else in Rust as the language is focused on these concepts of ownership and borrowing. Some of the material has already been discussed earlier, but here, we will strengthen that foundation. We will cover the following topics:

- Pointers and references
- Ownership and borrowing
- Boxes
- Reference counting

Trying out and experimenting with the examples is the key here as there are many concepts that you may not be familiar with yet.

Pointers and references

The *The stack and the heap* section of *Chapter 2, Using Variables and Types* gave us the basic information that we needed to understand memory layout of Rust. Let's recap the information and fill in some gaps.

The stack and the heap

When a program starts, by default a 2 MB chunk of memory called the stack is granted to it. The program will use its stack to store all its local variables and function parameters; for example, an i32 variable takes 4 bytes of the stack. When our program calls a function, a new stack frame is allocated to it. Through this mechanism, the stack knows the order in which the functions are called so that the functions return correctly to the calling code and possibly return values as well.

Dynamically sized types, such as strings or arrays, can't be stored on the stack. For these values, a program can request memory space on its heap, so this is a potentially much bigger piece of memory than the stack.

 When possible, stack allocation is preferred over heap allocation because accessing the stack is a lot more efficient.

Lifetimes

All variables in a Rust code have a lifetime. Suppose we declare an n variable with the let n = 42u32; binding. Such a value is valid from where it is declared to when it is no longer referenced, which is called the lifetime of the variable. This is illustrated in the following code snippet:

```
// see code in Chapter 6/code/lifetimes.rs
fn main() {
let n = 42u32;
let n2 = n; // a copy of the value from n to n2
life(n);
println!("{}", m);  // error: unresolved name `m`.
println!("{}", o);  // error: unresolved name `o`.
}

fn life(m: u32) -> u32 {
    let o = m;
    o
}
```

The lifetime of n ends when main() ends; in general, the start and end of a lifetime happen in the same scope. The words lifetime and scope are synonymous, but we generally use the word lifetime to refer to the extent of a reference. As in other languages, local variables or parameters declared in a function do not exist anymore after the function has finished executing; in Rust, we say that their lifetime has ended. This is the case for the m and o variables in the preceding code snippet, which are only known in the life function.

Likewise, the lifetime of a variable declared in a nested block is restricted to that block, like phi in the following example:

```
{
    let phi = 1.618;
}
println!("The value of phi is {}", phi); // is error
```

Trying to use phi when its lifetime is over results in an error: unresolved name 'phi'.

The lifetime of a value can be indicated in the code by an annotation, for example 'a, which reads as lifetime where a is simply an indicator; it could also be written as 'b, 'n, or 'life. It's common to see single letters being used to represent lifetimes. In the preceding example, an explicit lifetime indication was not necessary since there were no references involved. All values tagged with the same lifetime have the same maximum lifetime. We already know this notation from 'static, which, as we saw in the *Global constants* section of *Chapter 2, Using Variables and Types*, is the lifetime of things that last for the entire length of the program, so only use 'static when you need the value that long.

In the following example, we have a transform function that explicitly declares the lifetime of its s parameter to be 'a:

```
fn transform<'a>(s: &'a str) { /* ... */ }
```

Note the <'a> indication after the name of the function. In nearly all cases, this explicit indication is not needed because the compiler is smart enough to deduce the lifetimes, so we can simply write this:

```
fn transform_without_lifetime(s: &str) { /* ... */ }
```

Here is an example where even when we indicate a lifetime specifier 'a, the compiler does not allow our code. Let's suppose that we define a Magician struct as follows:

```
struct Magician {
  name: &'static str,
  power: u32
}
```

We will get an error message if we try to construct the following function:

```
fn return_magician<'a>() -> &'a Magician {
  let mag = Magician { name: "Gandalf", power: 4625};
  &mag
}
```

The error message is error: 'mag' does not live long enough. Why does this happen? The lifetime of the mag value ends when the return_magician function ends, but this function nevertheless tries to return a reference to the Magician value, which no longer exists. Such an invalid reference is known as a *dangling pointer*. This is a situation that would clearly lead to errors and cannot be allowed.

The lifespan of a pointer must always be shorter than or equal to than that of the value which it points to, thus avoiding dangling (or null) references.

In some situations, the decision to determine whether the lifetime of an object has ended is complicated, but in almost all cases, the borrow checker does this for us automatically by inserting lifetime annotations in the intermediate code; so, we don't have to do it. This is known as *lifetime elision*.

For example, when working with structs, we can safely assume that the struct instance and its fields have the same lifetime. Only when the borrow checker is not completely sure, we need to indicate the lifetime explicitly; however, this happens only on rare occasions, mostly when references are returned.

One example is when we have a struct with fields that are references. The following code snippet explains this:

```
struct MagicNumbers {
    magn1: &u32,
    magn2: &u32
}
```

This won't compile and will give us the following error: `missing lifetime specifier [E0106]`.

Therefore, we have to change the code as follows:

```
struct MagicNumbers<'a> {
    magn1: &'a u32,
    magn2: &'a u32
}
```

This specifies that both the struct and the fields have the lifetime as `'a`.

Perform the following exercise:

Explain why the following code won't compile:

```
// see code in Chapter 6/exercises/dangling_pointer.rs:
fn main() {
    let m: &u32 = {
        let n = &5u32;
        &*n
    };
    let o = *m;
}
```

Answer the same question for this code snippet as well:

```
let mut x = &3;
{
    let mut y = 4;
    x = &y;
}
```

Copying values and the Copy trait

In the code that we discussed in earlier section (see `Chapter 6/code/lifetimes.rs`) the value of n is copied to a new location each time n is assigned via a new `let` binding or passed as a function argument:

```
let n = 42u32;
// no move, only a copy of the value:
let n2 = n;
life(n);
fn life(m: u32) -> u32 {
    let o = m;
    o
}
```

At a certain moment in the program's execution, we would have four memory locations that contain the copied value 42, which we can visualize as follows:

```
STACK
        n    42
        n2   42
        m    42
        o    42
```

Each value disappears (and its memory location is freed) when the lifetime of its corresponding variable ends, which happens at the end of the function or code block in which it is defined. Nothing much can go wrong with this *Copy* behavior, in which the value (its bits) is simply copied to another location on the stack. Many built-in types, such as u32 and i64, work similar to this, and this copy-value behavior is defined in Rust as the Copy trait, which u32 and i64 implement.

You can also implement the `Copy` trait for your own type, provided all of its fields or items implement `Copy`. For example, the `MagicNumber` struct, which contains a field of the `u64` type, can have the same behavior. There are two ways to indicate this:

- One way is to explicitly name the `Copy` implementation as follows:

```
struct MagicNumber {
    value: u64
}
impl Copy for MagicNumber {}
```

- Otherwise, we can annotate it with a `Copy` attribute:

```
#[derive(Copy)]
struct MagicNumber {
    value: u64
}
```

This now means that we can create two different copies, `mag` and `mag2`, of a `MagicNumber` by assignment:

```
let mag = MagicNumber {value: 42};
let mag2 = mag;
```

They are copies because they have different memory addresses (the values shown will differ at each execution):

```
println!("{:?}", &mag as *const MagicNumber); // address is 0x23fa88
println!("{:?}", &mag2 as *const MagicNumber); // address is 0x23fa80
```

The (`*const` function is a so-called raw pointer; refer to *Chapter 9, Programming at the Boundaries* for more details about it). A type that does not implement the `Copy` trait is called non-copyable.

Another way to accomplish this is by letting `MagicNumber` implement the `Clone` trait:

```
#[derive(Clone)]
struct MagicNumber {
    value: u64
}
```

Then, we can use `clone()` `mag` into a different object called `mag3`, effectively making a copy as follows:

```
let mag3 = mag.clone();
println!("{:?}", &mag3 as *const MagicNumber); // address is 0x23fa78
```

`mag3` is a new pointer referencing a new copy of the value of `mag`.

Pointers

The n variable in the `let n = 42i32;` binding is stored on the stack. Values on the stack or the heap can be accessed by pointers. A pointer is a variable that contains the memory address of some value. To access the value it points to, dereference the pointer with `*`. This happens automatically in simple cases such as in `println!` or when a pointer is given as a parameter to a method. For example, in the following code, m is a pointer containing the address of n:

```
// see code in Chapter 6/code/references.rs:
let m = &n;
println!("The address of n is {:p}", m);
println!("The value of n is {}", *m);
println!("The value of n is {}", m);
```

This prints out the following output, which differs for each program run:

```
The address of n is 0x23fb34
The value of n is 42
The value of n is 42
```

So, why do we need pointers? When we work with dynamically allocated values, such as a `String`, that can change in size, the memory address of that value is not known at compile time. Due to this, the memory address needs to be calculated at runtime. So, to be able to keep track of it, we need a pointer for it whose value will change when the location of `String` in memory changes.

The compiler automatically takes care of the memory allocation of pointers and the freeing up of memory when their lifetime ends. You don't have to do this yourself like in C/C++, where you could mess up by freeing memory at the wrong moment or at multiple times.

The incorrect use of pointers in languages such as C++ leads to all kinds of problems.

However, Rust enforces a strong set of rules at compile time called the borrow checker, so we are protected against them. We have already seen them in action, but from here onwards, we'll explain the logic behind their rules.

Pointers can also be passed as arguments to functions, and they can be returned from functions, but the compiler severely restricts their usage.

When passing a pointer value to a function, it is always better to use the reference-dereference `&*` mechanism, as shown in this example:

```
let q = &42;
println!("{}", square(q)); // 1764
```

```
fn square(k: &i32) -> i32 {
    *k * *k
}
```

Rust has many kinds of pointers, which we will explore in this chapter. All pointers (except raw pointers, which are discussed in *Chapter 9, Programming at the Boundaries*) are guaranteed to be non-null (that is, they point to a valid location in the memory) and are automatically cleaned up.

References

In our previous example, m, which had the &n value, is the simplest form of pointer, and it is called a reference (or borrowed pointer); m is a reference to the stack-allocated n variable and has the &i32 type because it points to a value of the i32 type.

 In general, when n is a value of the T type, then the &n reference is of the &T type.

Here, n is immutable, so m is also immutable; for example, if you try to change the value of n through m with *m = 7; you will get a cannot assign to immutable borrowed content '*m' error. Contrary to C, Rust does not let you change an immutable variable via its pointer.

Since there is no danger of changing the value of n through a reference, multiple references to an immutable value are allowed; they can only be used to read the value, for example:

```
let o = &n;
println!("The address of n is {:p}", o);
println!("The value of n is {}", *o);
```

It prints out as described earlier:

```
The address of n is 0x23fb34
The value of n is 42
```

We could represent this situation in the memory as follows:

It is clear that working with pointers such as this or in much more complex situations necessitates much stricter rules than the `Copy` behavior. For example, the memory can only be freed when there are no variables or pointers associated with it anymore. And when the value is mutable, can it be changed through any of its pointers? These stricter rules, described by the ownership and borrowing system discussed in the next section, are enforced by the compiler.

Mutable references do exist, and they are declared as `let m = &mut n`. However, `n` also has to be a mutable value. When `n` is immutable, the compiler rejects the `m` mutable reference binding with the error, `cannot borrow immutable local variable 'n' as mutable`. This makes sense since immutable variables cannot be changed even when you know their memory location.

To reiterate, in order to change a value through a reference, both the variable and its reference have to be mutable, as shown in the following code snippet:

```
let mut u = 3.14f64;
let v = &mut u;
*v = 3.15;
println!("The value of u is now {}", *v);
```

This will print: `The value of u is now 3.15`.

Now, the value at the memory location of `u` is changed to `3.15`.

However, note that we now cannot change (or even print) that value anymore by using the `u`: `u = u * 2.0;` variable gives us a compiler error: `cannot assign to 'u' because it is borrowed` (we explain why this is so in the *Ownership and Borrowing* section of this chapter). We say that borrowing a variable (by making a reference to it) freezes that variable; the original `u` variable is frozen (and no longer usable) until the reference goes out of scope.

In addition, we can only have one mutable reference: `let w = &mut u;` which results in the error: `cannot borrow 'u' as mutable more than once at a time`. The compiler even adds the following note to the previous code line with: `let v = &mut u;` note: `previous borrow of 'u' occurs here; the mutable borrow prevents subsequent moves, borrows, or modification of 'u' until the borrow ends`. This is logical; the compiler is (rightfully) concerned that a change to the value of `u` through one reference might change its memory location because `u` might change in size, so it will not fit anymore within its previous location and would have to be relocated to another address. This would render all other references to `u` as invalid, and even dangerous, because through them we might inadvertently change another variable that has taken up the previous location of `u`!

A mutable value can also be changed by passing its address as a mutable reference to a function, as shown in this example:

```
let mut m = 7;
add_three_to_magic(&mut m);
println!("{}", m);   // prints out 10
```

With the function add_three_to_magic declared as follows:

```
fn add_three_to_magic(num: &mut i32) {
    *num += 3;   // value is changed in place through +=
}
```

To summarize, when n is a mutable value of the T type, then only one mutable reference to it (of the &mut T type) can exist at any time. Through this reference, the value can be changed.

Using ref in a match

If you want to get a reference to a matched variable inside a match function, use the ref keyword, as shown in the following example:

```
// see code in Chapter 6/code/ref.rs
fn main() {
    let n = 42;
    match n {
        ref r => println!("Got a reference to {}", r),
    }
    let mut m = 42;
    match m {
        ref mut mr => {
            println!("Got a mutable reference to {}", mr);
            *mr = 43;
        },
    }
    println!("m has changed to {}!", m);
}
```

Which prints out:

```
Got a reference to 42
Got a mutable reference to 42
m has changed to 43!
```

The `r` variable inside the `match` has the `&i32` type. In other words, the `ref` keyword creates a reference for use in the pattern. If you need a mutable reference, use `ref mut`.

We can also use `ref` to get a reference to a field of a struct or tuple in a destructuring via a `let` binding. For example, while reusing the `Magician` struct, we can extract the name of `mag` by using `ref` and then return it from the match:

```
let mag = Magician { name: "Gandalf", power: 4625};
let name = {
    let Magician { name: ref ref_to_name, power: _ } = mag;
    *ref_to_name
};
println!("The magician's name is {}", name);
```

Which prints: `The magician's name is Gandalf.`

References are the most common pointer type and have the most possibilities; other pointer types should only be applied in very specific use cases.

Ownership and borrowing

In the previous section, the word *borrowed* was mentioned in most error messages. What's this all about? What is the logic behind this borrow-checker mechanism?

Every program, whatever it does, whether reading data from a database or making a computation, is concerned with handling resources. The most common resource in a program is the memory space allocated to its variables. Other resources could be files, network connections, database connections, and so on. Every resource is given a name when we make a binding to it with `let`; in Rust's language, we say that the resource gets an owner, for example, in the following code snippet, `klaatu` owns a piece of memory that is taken up by the `Alien` struct instance:

```
// see code in Chapter 6/code/ownership1.rs
struct Alien {
  planet: String,
  n_tentacles: u32
}

fn main() {
  let mut klaatu = Alien{ planet: "Venus".to_string(),
  n_tentacles: 15 };
}
```

Only the owner can change the object it points to, and there can only be one owner at a time, because the owner is responsible for freeing the object's resources. When a reference goes out of scope, it will not deallocate the underlying memory, because the reference is not the owner of the value. This makes sense; if an object could have many owners, its resources could be freed more than once, which would lead to problems. When the owner's lifetime has passed, the compiler frees the memory automatically.

The owner can move the ownership of the object to another variable as follows:

```
let kl2 = klaatu;
```

Here, the ownership has moved from `klaatu` to `kl2`, but no data is actually copied. The original owner `klaatu` cannot be used anymore:

```
println!("{}", klaatu.planet);
```

It gives the compiler error as: `use of moved value 'klaatu.planet'`.

On the other hand, we can borrow the resource by making a (in this example mutable) reference `kl2` to `klaatu` with `let kl2 = &mut klaatu;`. A borrow is a temporary reference that passes the address of the data structure through `&`.

Now, `kl2` can change the object, for instance, when our alien loses a tentacle in a battle:

```
kl2.n_tentacles = 14;
println!("{} - {}", kl2.planet, kl2.n_tentacles);
```

This prints out: `Venus - 14`.

However, we will get an error message if we try to change the alien's planet through the following code:

```
klaatu.planet = "Pluto".to_string();
```

The error message is `error: cannot assign to ` + "`klaatu.planet`" + ` because it is borrowed`; it was indeed borrowed by `kl2`. Similar to everyday life, while an object is borrowed, the owner does not have access to it as it is no longer in their possession. In order to change the resource, `klaatu` needs to own it, without the resource being borrowed at the same time.

Rust even explains this to us with the note that it adds: `borrow of 'klaatu.planet' occurs here ownership.rs:8    let kl2 = &mut klaatu;`.

Since `kl2` borrows the resource, Rust also even forbids us to access the instance with its former name, `klaatu`:

```
println!("{} - {}", klaatu.planet, klaatu.n_tentacles);
```

The compiler then throws this error message: `error: cannot borrow 'klaatu.planet' as immutable because 'klaatu' is also borrowed as mutable`.

When a resource is moved or borrowed, the previous owner can no longer use it. This prevents the memory problem that is known as a dangling pointer, which is the use of a pointer that points to an invalid memory location.

But here is a revelation: if we isolate the borrowing by `kl2` in its own block, as follows:

```
// see code in Chapter 6/code/ownership2.rs
fn main() {
  let mut klaatu = Alien{ planet: "Venus".to_string(), n_tentacles: 15
};
  {
    let kl2 = &mut klaatu;
    kl2).n_tentacles = 14;
    println!("{} - {}", kl2.planet, kl2.n_tentacles);
// prints: Venus - 14
  }
}
```

The former problems have disappeared! After the block, we can now do for example:

```
    println!("{} - {}", klaatu.planet, klaatu.n_tentacles);  klaatu.
planet = "Pluto".to_string();
    println!("{} - {}", klaatu.planet, klaatu.n_tentacles);
```

This prints:

```
Venus - 10
Pluto - 10.
```

Why does this happen? Because after the closing } of the code block in which `kl2` was bound, its lifetime ended. The borrowing was over (a borrow has to end sometime) and `klaatu` reclaimed full ownership, and thus the right to change. When the compiler detects that the lifetime of the original owner, `klaatu`, has eventually ended, the memory occupied by the struct instance is automatically freed.

In fact, this is a general rule in Rust; whenever an object goes out of scope and it doesn't have an owner anymore, its destructor is automatically called and the resources owned by it are freed so that there can never be any memory (or other resource) leaks. In other words, Rust obeys the **Resource Acquisition Is Initialization (RAII)** rule. For more information, go to `http://en.wikipedia.org/wiki/Resource_Acquisition_Is_Initialization`.

As we experimented in the *References* section, a resource can be immutably borrowed many times, but while it is immutably borrowed, the original data can't be mutably borrowed.

Another way to move a resource (and transfer the ownership) is to pass it as an argument to a function; try this out in the following exercise:

- Examine the situation (`let k12 = &klaatu;`) when `k12` is not a mutable reference. Can you change the instance through `k12`? Can you change the instance through `klaatu`? Explain the error with what you know about ownership and borrowing (refer to `Chapter 6/exercises/ownership3.rs`).

- What will happen in the previous program if we do `let klaatuc = klaatu;` before we define the `let k12 = &klaatu;` binding?

- Examine if you can change the mutability of a resource by moving from an immutable owner to a mutable owner.

- For our `Alien` struct, write a `grow_a_tentacle` method that increases the number of tentacles by one (refer to `Chapter 6/exercises/grow_a_tentacle.rs`).

Boxes

Another pointer type in Rust is called the boxed pointer, `Box<T>`, which can be defined for a value of a generic `T` type. A box is a non-copyable value. This pointer type is used to allocate objects on the heap. For example, here we allocate an `Alien` value on the heap by using the following code:

```
// see code in Chapter 6/code/boxes1.rs
let mut a1 = Box::new(Alien{ planet: "Mars".to_string(), n_tentacles:
4 });
println!("{}", a1.n_tentacles); // 4
```

The `a1` variable is the only owner of this memory resource that may read from and write to it.

We can make a reference to the value pointed to by the box pointer, and if both the original box and this new reference are mutable, we can change the object through this reference:

```
let a2 = &mut a1;
println!("{}", a2.planet ); // Mars
a2.n_tentacles = 5;
```

After such a borrowing, the usual ownership rules as specified earlier hold, since a1 no longer has access, not even for reading:

```
// error: cannot borrow `a1.n_tentacles` as immutable because `a1` is
also borrowed as mutable
// println!("{}", a1.n_tentacles); // is error!
// error: cannot assign to `a1.planet` because it is borrowed
a1.planet = "Pluto".to_string();   // is error!
```

We can also use this mechanism to put simple values on the heap as follows:

```
let n = Box::new(42);
```

As always, n points by default to an immutable value and any attempt to change this with:

```
*n = 67;
```

Provokes the error: cannot assign to immutable 'Box' content '*n'.

Another reference can also point to the dereferenced Box value:

```
let q = &*n;
println!("{}", q); // 42
```

In the following example, we again see a boxed value pointed to by n, but the ownership of the value is now given to a mutable pointer, m:

```
// see code in Chapter 6/code/boxes2.rs
let n = Box::new(42);
let mut m = n;
*m = 67;
// println!("{}", n); // error: use of moved value: `n`
println!("{}", m); // 67
```

By dereferencing m and assigning a new value to m, this value is entered into the memory location that was originally pointed to by n. Of course, n cannot be used anymore; we get the error: use of moved value: 'n' message because n is no longer the owner of the value.

Here is another example where the ownership has clearly has moved from a1 to a2:

```
let mut a1 = Box::new(Alien{ planet: "Mars".to_string(), n_tentacles:
4 });
let a2 = a1;
println!("{}", a2.n_tentacles); // 4
```

No data being copied here, except the address of the struct value. After the move, a1 can no longer be used to access the data, and a2 is responsible for freeing the memory.

If a2 is given as an argument to a function such as use_alien in the following code snippet, a2 also gives up the ownership, which is then transferred to the function:

```
use_alien(a2);
// Following line gives the error: use of moved value: `a2.n_
tentacles`
// println!("{}", a2.n_tentacles);
} // end of main() function

fn use_alien(a: Box<Alien>) {
    println!("An alien from planet {} is freed after the closing brace",
    a.planet);
}
```

This prints out: An alien from planet Mars is freed.

Indeed, when use_alien() has finished executing, the memory allocation for that value is freed. However, in general, you must always let your function take a simple reference as a parameter (in a similar way to the square function explained earlier), rather than take a parameter of the Box type. We could improve our example by calling a use_alien2 function as follows:

```
fn use_alien2(a: &Alien) {
    println!("An alien from planet {} is freed", a.planet);
}
```

And calling it with: use_alien2(&*a2);.

Sometimes, your program may need to manipulate a recursive data structure that refers to itself, as shown in the following struct:

```
struct Recurs {
    list: Vec<u8>,          .
    rec_list: Option<Box<Recurs>>
}
```

This represents a list of lists of bytes. The rec_list function is either a Some<Box<Recurs>> function containing a Box pointer to another list or a None value, which means that the list of lists ends there. Since the number of items in this list (and thus its size) is only known at runtime such structures must be always constructed as a Box type. For other use cases, you must prefer references over Boxes.

Reference counting

Sometimes, you need several references to an immutable value at the same time; this is also called shared ownership. `Box<T>` can't help us out here because this type has a single owner by definition. For this, Rust provides the generic reference counted box, `Rc<T>`, where multiple references can share the same resource. The `std::rc` module provides a way to share ownership of the same value between different `Rc` pointers; the value remains alive as long as there is least one pointer referencing it.

In the following example, we have aliens that have a number of tentacles. Each `Tentacle` has to indicate to which `Alien` it belongs; besides this, it also has other properties (such as a degree of poison), so we define it also as a struct. A first attempt at this could be the following code, which however does not compile (from `Chapter 6/code/refcount_not_good.rs`):

```
struct Alien {
    name: String,
    n_tentacles: u8
}

struct Tentacle {
    poison: u8,
    owner: Alien
}

fn main() {
let dhark = Alien { name: "Dharkalen".to_string(), n_tentacles: 7 };
    // defining dhark's tentacles:
    for i in 1u8..dhark.n_tentacles {
        Tentacle { poison: i * 3, owner: dhark }; // <- error!
    }
}
```

The compiler gives the following error for the line in the for loop: `error: use of moved value 'dhark' - note: 'dhark' moved here because it has type 'Alien', which is non-copyable.`

When it is defined, each `Alien` `Tentacle` seemingly tries to make a copy of the `Alien` instance as its owner, which makes no sense and is not allowed.

The correct version defines the owner in the `Tentacle` struct to have the `Rc<Alien>` type:

```
// see code in Chapter 6/code/refcount.rs
use std::rc::Rc;
#[derive(Debug)]
```

```
struct Alien {
    name: String,
    n_tentacles: u8
}
#[derive(Debug)]
struct Tentacle {
    poison: u8,
    owner: Rc<Alien>
}

fn main() {
    let dhark = Alien { name: "Dharkalen".to_string(), no_tentacles: 7
};
    let dhark_master = Rc::new(dhark);
    for i in 1u8..dhark_master.n_tentacles {
        let t = Tentacle { poison: i * 3, owner: dhark_master.clone() };
        println!("{:?}", t);
    }
}
```

This prints the following:

```
Tentacle { poison: 3, owner: Alien { name: "Dharkalen", n_tentacles: 7
} }
Tentacle { poison: 6, owner: Alien { name: "Dharkalen", n_tentacles: 7
} }
...
Tentacle { poison: 18, owner: Alien { name: "Dharkalen", n_tentacles:
7 } }
```

We envelop our `Alien` instance in an `Rc<T>` type with `Rc::new(dhark)`. Applying the `clone()` method on this `Rc` object provides each `Tentacle` with its own reference to the `Alien` object. Note that `clone()` here copies the `Rc` pointer, not the `Alien` struct. We also annotate the structs with `#[derive(Debug)]` so that we can print out their instances through a `println!("{:?}", t);`.

If we want mutability inside our `Rc` type, we have to either use a *Cell* pointer if the value implements the *Copy* trait or a *RefCell* pointer. Both these smart pointers are found in the `std:cell` module.

However, the `Rc` pointer type can only be used inside one thread of execution. If you need shared ownership across multiple threads, you need to use the `Arc<T>` pointer (short for **atomic reference counted box**), which is the thread-safe counterpart of `Rc` (refer to the *Atomic reference counting* section of *Chapter 8, Concurrency and Parallelism*).

An overview of pointers

In the following table, we summarize the different pointers used in Rust. T represents a generic type. We haven't yet encountered the Arc, *const, and *mut pointers, but they are included here for completeness.

Pointers	Pointer names	Description
&T	Reference	This allows one or more references to read T.
&mut T	Mutable reference	This allows a single reference to read and write T.
Box<T>	Box	This is a heap-allocated T with a single owner that may read and write T.
Rc<T>	Rc pointer	This is a heap-allocated T with many readers.
Arc<T>	Arc pointer	This is like Rc<T>, but enables safe mutable sharing across threads (refer to *Chapter 8, Concurrency and Parallelism*).
*const T	Raw pointer	This allows unsafe read access to T (refer to *Chapter 9, Programming at the Boundaries*).
*mut T	Mutable raw pointer	This allows unsafe read and write access to T (refer to *Chapter 9, Programming at the Boundaries*).

Summary

In this chapter, we learned the intelligence behind the Rust compiler, which is embodied in the principles of ownership, moving values, and borrowing. We saw the different pointers that Rust advocates: references, boxes, and reference counters. Now that we have a grasp on how this all works together, we will understand the errors, warnings, and messages the compiler may throw at us in a much better way.

In the following chapter, we will expose the bigger units of code organization in code, such as modules and crates, and how we can write macros to make coding less repetitive.

7
Organizing Code and Macros

We start this chapter by discussing the large-scale code-organizing structures in Rust, namely modules and crates. We will look at the following topics:

- Building crates
- Defining a module
- Visibility of items
- Importing modules and file hierarchy
- Importing external crates
- Exporting a public interface
- Adding external crates to a project
- The test module

We will also touch upon how to build macros in order to generate code and save time and effort, particularly in these topics:

- The reason for using macros
- Developing macros
- Using macros from crates

Modules and crates

Until now, we only looked at the situation where our code fitted in one file. However, when a project evolves, we will want to split the code across several files, for example, if we put all the data structures and methods that describe a certain functionality in the same file, how will the main code file be able to call these functions in other files?

In addition, when we start using multiple functions in varied files, it sometimes happens that we want to use the same name for two different functions. How can we properly differentiate between such functions? How can we make it so that some functions are callable everywhere and others are not? For this, we need what other languages call namespaces and access modifiers; in Rust, this is done through the module system.

Building crates

At the highest level of building crates, there is the crate. The Rust distribution contains a number of crates, such as the `std` crate of the standard library, which we have already used often. Other built-in crates are the `collections` crate, with the functionality to work with strings, vectors, lists, and key-value maps, and the `test` crate, with unit-testing and micro-benchmarking functionalities.

A crate is the equivalent of a package or library in other languages. It is also the unit of compilation; `rustc` only compiles one crate at a time. What does this mean? When our project has a code file containing a `main()` function, then it is clear that our project is an executable program (which is also called a binary) that starts execution in `main()`. For example, if we compile `structs.rs` as `rustc structs.rs`, a `.exe` file `structs.exe` will be produced in Windows (and equivalent formats on other operating systems) that can be executed on its own. This is the standard behavior when you invoke `rustc`. When working with Cargo (refer to *Chapter 1, Starting with Rust*), we have to indicate that we want a binary project at its creation with the `--bin` flag: `cargo new projname --bin`.

However, often your intention is to write a project whose code will be called from other projects, a so-called shared library (this is a `.dll` file in Windows, a `.so` file in Linux, and a `.dylib` file in Mac OS X.) In this case, your code will only contain the data structures and functions to work on them. Then, you must explicitly indicate this to the compiler using the `--crate-type` flag with the `lib` option: `rustc --crate-type=lib structs.rs`.

The resulting file is far smaller in size and is called `libstructs.rlib`; the suffix is now `.rlib` (for the Rust library) and `lib` is prepended before the filename. If you want the crate to have another name such as `mycrate`, then use the `--crate-name` flag as follows:

```
rustc --crate-type=lib --crate-name=mycrate structs.rs
```

This creates a `libmycrate.rlib` as the output file. An alternative to using the `rustc` flags is to put this information as an attribute at the top of the code file, as follows:

```
// from Chapter 7/code/structs.rs
#![crate_type = "lib"]
#![crate_name = "mycrate"]
```

The `crate_type` attribute can take the `bin`, `lib`, `rlib`, `dylib`, or `staticlib` values, according to whether you want an executable binary or a library of a certain type that is dynamic or statically linked. (In general, when an `attr` attribute applies to a whole crate, the syntax to use in the code is `#![crate_attr]`.)

Each library used in an application is a separate crate. In any case, you need an executable (binary) crate that uses the library crates.

Cargo's job is to handle crates (for more information on Cargo, refer to the *Working with Cargo* section of *Chapter 1, Starting with Rust*); it creates a library project by default. You can install other crates into your project from the crates repository at `https://crates.io`; in the *Adding external crates to a project* section of this chapter, we will see how this is done.

Defining a module

Crates are the compiled entities that get distributed on machines to execute. All of the code of a crate is contained in an implicit root module. This code can then be split up by the developer into code units called modules, which in fact, form a hierarchy of submodules under the root module. This way the organization of our code can be greatly improved. An evident candidate for a module is the test code—we'll use this in the *The test module* section.

Modules can also be defined inside other modules as the so-called nested modules. Modules do not get compiled individually; only crates get compiled. All the module's code is inserted into the crate's source file before compilation starts.

In the previous chapters, we used built-in modules, such as `io`, `str`, and `vec` from the `std` crate. The `std` crate contains many modules and functions that are used in real projects; the most common types, traits, functions, and macros (such as `println!`) are declared in the prelude module.

A module typically contains a collection of code items such as traits, structs, methods, other functions, and even nested modules. The module's name defines a namespace for all the objects that it contains. We define a module with the mod keyword and a lowercase name (such as game1) as follows:

```
mod game1 {
    // all of the module's code items go in here
}
```

Similar as in Java each file is a module, for every code file the compiler defines an implicit module, even when it does not contain the mod keyword. As we will see in the *Importing modules and file hierarchy* section, such a code file can be imported into the current code file with mod filename. Suppose game1 is the name of a module that contains a func2 function. If you want to use this function in a code that is external to this module, you would address it as game1::func2. However, whether this is possible will depend on the visibility of func2.

The visibility of items

Items in a module are by default, only visible in the module itself; they are private to the module. If you want to make an item callable from a code that is external to the module, you must explicitly indicate this by prefixing the item with pub (which stands for public). In the following code, trying to call func1() is not allowed by the compiler: error: function `func1` is private:.

```
// from Chapter 7/code/modules.rs
mod game1 {
    // all of the module's code items go in here
    fn func1() {
        println!("Am I visible?");
    }
    pub fn func2() {
        println!("You called func2 in game1!");
    }
}

fn main() {
    // game1::func1(); // <- error!
    game1::func2();
}
```

However, if you call func2(), it will work without any problem because it is public, and this prints out: You called func2 in game1!

A function in a nested module can only be called if it is public, provided the nested module itself is declared public, as shown in this code snippet:

```
mod game1 {
    // other code
    pub mod subgame1 {
        pub fn subfunc1() {
            println!("You called subfunc1 in subgame1!");
        }
    }
}

fn main() {
    // other code
    game1::subgame1::subfunc1();
}
```

It prints out: `You called subfunc1 in subgame1!`

A function in a module must be prefixed with its module name when it is called. This distinguishes it from another function with the same name so that no name conflicts occur.

When a struct is accessed from outside the module in which it is defined, it is only visible when it is declared with `pub`. Moreover, its fields are private by default, so you have to explicitly declare as `pub` the fields that you want to be visible outside. This is the encapsulation property (also called information hiding) from traditional object-oriented languages. In the following example, the name and age fields of the `Magician` struct belong to the public interface but `power` does not:

```
pub struct Magician {
    pub name: String,
    pub age: i32,
    power: i32
}
```

So this statement:

```
let mag1 = game1::Magician { name: "Gandalf".to_string(), age: 725,
power: 98};
```

This leads to the compiler error: `field 'power' of struct 'game1::Magician' is private`

Perform the following exercise:

Does this mean that we cannot make instances from a struct with private fields? Try to think of a way around this. (As a hint, think about a constructor-like `new` function; refer to `Chapter 7/code/priv_struct.rs`.)

Importing modules and file hierarchy

The use keyword in use game1::func2; imports a func2 function from the game1 module so that it can be simply called with its name, func2(). You can even give it a shorter name with use game1::func2 as gf2; so that it can be called as gf2().

When the game1 module contains two (or more) functions such as func2 and func3 that we want to import, this can be done with use game1::{func2, func3};.

If you want to import all the (public) functions of the game1 module, you can do it with *: use game1::*;.

However, using such a global import is not the best practice, except in modules for testing. The main reason for this is that a global import makes it harder to see where names are bound. Furthermore, they are forwards-incompatible, since new upstream exports can clash with existing names.

Inside a module, self:: and super:: can be prepended to a path similar to game1::func2 to distinguish between a function in the current module itself and a function in the parent scope, outside of the module. The use statements are preferably written at the top of the code file, so that they work for the whole of the code.

In the previous example, the module was defined in the main source file itself; in most cases, a module will be defined in another source file. So, how do we import such modules? In Rust, we can insert the entire contents of a module's source file into the current file by declaring the module at the top of the code (but after any use statements) like this: mod modul1;, this can be optionally preceded by pub. This statement will look for a modul1.rs file in the same folder as the current source file and import its code within the current code inside a modul1 module. If a modul1.rs file is not found, it will look for a mod.rs file in the modul1 subfolder and insert its code.

Here is a simple import_modules.rs example that contains the following code:

```
// from Chapter 7/code/import_modules.rs
mod modul1;
mod modul2;
fn main() {
  modul1::func1();
  modul2::func1();
}
```

In the `modul1` subfolder, we have the `mod.rs` file that contains the following code snippet:

```
pub fn func1() {
    println!("called func1 from modul1");
}
```

The `modul2.rs` file in the same folder as `import_modules.rs` contains the following code:

```
pub fn func1() {
    println!("called func1 from modul2");
}
```

 Note that these source files of the module don't contain the `mod` declaration anymore because they were already declared in `import_modules.rs`.

Executing `import_modules` prints out the following output: `called func1 from modul1` and `called func1 from modul2`.

What happens if you simply call `func1()` in `main()`? Now, the compiler doesn't know which `func1` to call, from `modul1` or from `modul2`, resulting in the error: `unresolved name 'func1'` message. However, if we add `use modul1::func1` and then call `func1()`, it will work as the ambiguity is resolved.

Importing external crates

In the *Traits* section of *Chapter 5, Generalizing Code with Higher-order Functions and Parametrization*, we developed the `traits.rs` structs for `Alien`, `Zombie`, and `Predator` characters that implemented a `Monster` trait. The code file contained a `main()` function to make it executable. We will now incorporate this code (without the `main()` part) in a library project called monsters and see how we can call this code.

Create the project with cargo new monsters and create a folder structure in the `monsters/src/lib.rs` file with the `template` code:

```
#[test]
fn it_works() {
}
```

Remove this code and replace it with the code from `traits.rs`, but omit the `main()` function. In addition, add a simple `print_from_monsters()` function to test whether you can call it from the library:

```
// from Chapter 7/code/monsters/src/lib.rs:
fn print_from_monsters() {
    println!("Printing from crate monsters!");
}
```

Then, compile the library with cargo build, producing a `libmonsters-hash.rlib` library file in the `target/debug` folder (where hash is a random string similar to `547968b7c0a4d435`).

Now, we create a `main.rs` file in the `src` folder to make an executable file that can call into our `monsters` library and copy the original `main()` code from `traits.rs` in it, adding a call to `print_from_monsters()`:

```
// from Chapter 7/code/monsters/src/main.rs:
fn main() {
    print_from_monsters();
    let zmb1 = Zombie {health: 75, damage: 15};
    println!("Oh no, I hear: {}", zmb1.noise());
    zmb1.attack();
    println!("{:?}", zmb1);
}
```

 This is a common design pattern—a library project containing an executable program that can be used to demonstrate or test the library.

The `cargo build` function will now compile both the projects if there are no problems. However, the code will not compile, and the compiler will give the error: `unresolved name 'print_from_monsters'` message, clearly the code for the function is not found.

The first thing that we have to do is make the library code available to our program, which can be done by placing the following statement at the start:

```
extern crate monsters;
```

This statement will import all the (public) items contained in the crate monsters under a module with the same name. However, this is not enough; we must also indicate that the `print_from_monsters` function can be found in the `monsters` module. Indeed, the monsters crate creates an implicit module with the same name. So, we have to call our function as follows:

```
monsters::print_from_monsters();
```

Now, we get the error: `function 'print_from_monsters' is private` message, which tells us that the function is found, but it is inaccessible. This is easy to fix. In the *Visibility of Items* section, we saw how to remedy this; we must prefix the function header with `pub`, as follows:

```
pub fn print_from_monsters() { … }
```

Now, this part of our code works! Open a terminal, go (`cd`) to the `target/debug` folder and start the monsters executable. This will give the output as `Printing from crate monsters!`.

You will see that `extern crate abc` (with `abc` a crate name) is often used in code, but you will never see `extern crate std`; why does this happen? The reason is that `std` is imported by default in every other crate. For the same reason, the contents of the prelude module are imported by default in to every module.

Exporting a public interface

The compiler throws the following error at us: `error: Zombie does not name a structure`. Clearly, the code for the `Zombie` struct is not found. Since this struct also resides in the monsters module, the solution to fix this is easy; prefix `Zombie` with `monsters::` as follows:

```
let zmb1 = monsters::Zombie {health: 75, damage: 15};
```

Another error: `struct 'Zombie' is private`, makes it clear that we must mark the `Zombie` struct with `pub`, that is, `pub struct Zombie { … }`.

Now, we will get an error on the line that contains `zmb1.noise()`: `error: type 'monsters::Zombie'` does not implement any method in scope named `'noise'`

The accompanying help note explains to us what to do and why we should do it: `help: methods from traits can only be called if the trait is in scope; the following trait is implemented but not in scope, perhaps add a 'use' for it:`

`help: candidate #1: use 'monsters::Monster'`. So, let's add this to the following code:

```
extern crate monsters;
use monsters::Monster;
```

The last error—`error: trait 'Monster' is private - source trait is private`— that we have to solve occurs at the `use` line. Again very logical; if we want to use a trait, it must be publicly visible: `pub trait Monster { ... }`.

Now, cargo build is successful, if we execute monsters the output will be as follows:

```
Printing from crate monsters!
Oh no, I hear: Aaargh!
The Zombie bites! Your health lowers with 30 damage points.
Zombie { health: 75, damage: 15 }
```

This makes it clear that the things we want to make visible in our module (or put in another way, that we want to export) must be annotated with `pub`; they form the interface that our module exposes to the outside world.

Adding external crates to a project

How to use libraries written by others (that is, choose from the multitude of libraries available at `https://crates.io`) in our project? Cargo makes this very easy.

Suppose we want to use both the `log` and the `mac` libraries in the monsters project. The `log` function is a simple logging framework by the Rust Project Developers that gives us a number of macros such as `info!`, `warn!`, and `trace!` to log information messages. The `mac` function is an amazing collection of useful macros, which is maintained by Jonathan Reem.

To get these libraries, we need to edit our `Cargo.toml` configuration file and add a `[dependencies]` section when it isn't already present. Beneath it, we specify the versions of the libraries that we want to use:

```
[dependencies]
log = "0.2.5"
mac = "*"
```

A `*` character denotes that any version is okay, and the most recent version will be installed.

Save the file and, in the `monsters` folder, issue the `cargo build` command. Cargo will take care of locally installing and compiling the libraries:

```
F:\monsters>cargo build
    Updating registry `https://github.com/rust-lang/crates.io-index`
Downloading mac v0.0.1
    Compiling log v0.2.5
    Compiling mac v0.0.1
    Compiling monsters v0.0.1 (file:///F:/monsters)
src\lib.rs:35:16: 35:27 warning: struct field is never used: `health`, #[warn(dea
d_code)] on by default
```

It will also automatically update the `Cargo.lock` file to register the installed versions of the libraries so that subsequent project builds will always use the same versions (here, `log v0.3.1` and `mac v0.0.1`). If you later want to update to the most recent version of a library, for example for the `log` library, do a cargo update `-p log` or a `cargo` update to update all libraries. This will download the latest crate versions for the crates that are indicated with the `*` version. If you want a higher version for a crate, change its version number in `Cargo.toml`.

Start using the libraries by importing their crates in the code:

```
#[macro_use]
extern crate log;
extern crate mac;
```

The `#[macro_use]` attribute allows the use of macros defined in the external crate. (See the next section for more information). Then, we can for example, use the `info!` macro from `crate mac` as follows:

```
info!("Gathering information from monster {:?}", zmb1);
```

The test module

Let's apply this code organization to a module that contains our tests. In a larger project, tests are separated from the application code as follows:

- Unit tests are collected in a `test` module
- Integration tests are collected in a `lib.rs` file in a `tests` directory

Let's make a concrete example by using our cube function from *Chapter 3, Using Functions and Control Structures*, and start its project with cargo new cube. We must replace the code in src\lib.rs with this:

```
// from Chapter 7/code/cube/src/lib.rs:
#[cfg(test)]
mod test;
pub fn cube(val: u32) -> u32 {
    // implementation goes here
    val * val * val
}
```

#[cfg(test)] ensures that the test module is only compiled when testing. In the second line, we declare our test module, which is preceded by the test attribute. The code of this module goes into a test.rs file in the same folder:

```
// from Chapter 7/code/cube/src/test.rs:
use super::*;
#[test]
fn cube_of_2_is_8() {
    assert_eq!(cube(2), 8);
}
// other test functions:
// ...
```

We need to use super::* to import all the functions that need to test; here, this is cube.

Integration tests go into a lib.rs file in a tests folder:

```
// from Chapter 7/code/cube/tests/lib.rs:
extern crate cube;
#[test]
fn cube_of_4_is_64() {
    assert_eq!(cube::cube(4), 64);
}
// other test functions:
// ...
```

Here, we need to import the cube crate with an extern command and qualify the cube function name with its module name, cube (or else do a use cube::cube;).

The test code will only be compiled and run when we give the `cargo test` command, which will give these results:

```
F:\Rust\Rust book\Chapter 7 - Organizing code and macros\code\cube>cargo test
    Compiling cube v0.0.1 (file:///F:/Rust/Rust%20book/Chapter%207%20-%20Organizin
g%20code%20and%20macros/code/cube)
    Running target\debug\cube-9df08137b1193fbc.exe

running 1 test
test test::cube_of_2_is_8 ... ok

test result: ok. 1 passed; 0 failed; 0 ignored; 0 measured

    Running target\debug\lib-96e9f24771964202.exe

running 1 test
test cube_of_4_is_64 ... ok

test result: ok. 1 passed; 0 failed; 0 ignored; 0 measured

   Doc-tests cube

running 0 tests

test result: ok. 0 passed; 0 failed; 0 ignored; 0 measured
```

We can see that our two tests passed. The end of the output also shows that tests in the documentation are also executed if they are present.

Macros

Macros are not new to you as we have already used them. Every time we called an expression that ended with an exclamation mark (`!`), we called a built-in macro; the `!` sign distinguishes it from a function. In our code until now, we have already used `println!`, `assert_eq!`, `panic!`, and `vec!` macros.

Why do we use macros?

Macros make powerful language or syntax extensions; therefore, they make metaprogramming possible. For example, Rust has a `regex!` macro that allows you to define regular expressions in your program, which are compiled while your code is compiled. This way the regular expressions are verified, they can be optimized at compile time, and there is no runtime overhead.

Macros can capture repetitive or resembling code patterns and replace them with other source code: the macro expands the original code into new code. This expansion happens early in compilation, before any static checking is done, so the resulting code is compiled together with the original code. In this sense, they resemble Lisp macros much more than C macros. Rust macros allow you to write **Don't Repeat Yourself (DRY)** code by factoring out the common parts of functions. However, a macro is at a higher level than a function because a macro allows you to generate the code for many functions at compile time.

A Rust developer can also write his/her own macros, replacing repetitive code with much simpler code and thereby automating tasks. On the other side of the spectrum, it could even make it possible to write domain-specific languages. Macro coding follows a specific set of declarative pattern-based rules. Rust's macro system is also hygienic, which means that no conflict is possible between the variables used in the macro and those outside the macro. Each macro expansion happens in a distinct syntax context, and each variable is tagged with the syntax context where it was introduced.

Macro code itself is harder to understand than normal Rust code, so it is not that easy to make. However, you won't code macros every day; if a macro is tested, just use it. The full story of macro writing extends into advanced regions of Rust, but in the following sections, we will discuss the basic techniques to develop macros.

Developing macros

The basic structure of a macro definition for a macro with the `mac1` name is of the following form:

```
macro_rules! mac1 {
    (pattern) => (expansion);
    (pattern) => (expansion);
    ...
}
```

The definition of a macro is also done through a macro, that is, the `macro_rules` macro! As you can see a macro is similar to a match block as it defines one or more rules for pattern matching, and each rule ends with a semicolon. Every rule consists of a pattern before the `=>` sign (which also called a matcher) that is replaced with the expansion part during compilation, and not while executing the code.

The following `welcome!` macro expects no pattern and expands into a print statement by using the `println!` macro; this is simple, but it demonstrates how macros work:

```
// from Chapter 7/code/macros.rs
macro_rules! welcome {
    () => (
        println!(""Welcome to the Game!");
    )
}
```

It is invoked by adding an exclamation sign (`!`) to its name:

```
fn main() {
  welcome!()
}
```

This prints out: `Welcome to the Game!`.

A matcher can contain an expression of the `$arg:frag` form:

- The `$arg` function binds an `arg` meta-variable to a value when the macro is called. Variables used inside a macro such as `$arg`, are prefixed with a $ sign to distinguish them from normal variables in the code.

- The `frag` function is a *fragment specifier* and can be either `expr`, `item`, `block`, `stmt`, `pat`, `ty` (type), `ident`, `path`, or `tt`.

(You can find more information on the meaning of these fragments in the official documentation at `http://doc.rust-lang.org/1.0.0/book/advanced-macros.html`.)

Any other Rust literals (tokens) that appear in a matcher must match exactly. For example, the following `mac1` macro:

```
macro_rules! mac1 {
    ($arg:expr) => (println!("arg is {}", $arg));
}
```

When you call `mac1!(42);`, it will print out `arg is 42`. The `mac1` function looks at its argument, `42`, as an expression (`expr`) and binds `arg` to the value.

Perform the following exercises:

- Write a `mac2` macro that triples its argument. Test it out for these arguments: 5 and 2 + 3.

- Write a `mac3` macro that takes an identifier name and replaces it with a binding of that name to 42. (As a hint, use `$arg:ident` instead of `$arg:expr;` ident is used for variable and function names.)

- Write a `mac4` macro that when invoked like `mac4!("Where am I?");`, prints out `start - Where am I? - end`. (Refer to the example code in `Chapter 7/exercises/macro_ex.rs`.)

Repetition

What would we do if there is more than one argument? We will enclose the pattern with a `$(...)*`, where `*` means zero or more (instead of `*`, you can use `+`, which means one or more). For example, the following `printall` macro invokes `println!` on each of its arguments, which can be of the arbitrary type and are separated by a:

```
macro_rules! printall {
    ( $( $arg:expr ), * ) => ( {$( print!("{} / ", $arg) ); *} );
}
```

When called with `printall!("hello", 42, 3.14);` it will print out: `hello / 42 / 3.14 /`.

In the example, each argument (separated by commas) is substituted by a corresponding invocation of `print!` that is separated by a `/`. Note that on the right-hand side, we have to make a code block of the resulting print statements by enclosing them in `{ }`.

Creating a new function

Here is a `create_fn` macro to create a new function at compile time:

```
macro_rules! create_fn {
    ($fname:ident) => (
        fn $fname() {
            println!("Called the function {:?}()", stringify!($fname))
        }
    )
}
```

The `stringify!` macro simply makes a string from its argument. Now, we can invoke this macro with `create_fn!(fn1);`. This statement does not sit inside `main()` or another function; it is transformed during compilation into the function definition. Then, a normal call to the `fn1()` function will call it, here printing `Called the function "fn1"()`.

In the following `massert` macro, we mimic the behavior of the `assert!` macro, which does nothing when its expression argument is true but panics when it is false:

```
macro_rules! massert {
    ($arg:expr) => (
            if $arg {}
            else { panic!("Assertion failed!"); }
    );
}
```

For example, `massert!(1 == 42);` will print out `thread '<main>' panicked at 'Assertion failed!'`.

In the following statements, we test whether the v vector contains certain elements:

```
let v = [10, 40, 30];
massert!(v.contains(&30));
massert!(!v.contains(&50));
```

The `unless` macro mimics an `unless` statement where a branch is executed if the `arg` condition is not true. For example:

```
unless!(v.contains(&25), println!("v does not contain 25"));
```

This should print out `v does not contain 25` because the condition is not true.

This is also a one-line macro:

```
macro_rules! unless {
    ($arg:expr, $branch:expr) => ( if !$arg { $branch }; );
}
```

The last example combines the techniques that we have seen so far. In the *Attributes - Testing* section of *Chapter 3, Using Functions and Control Structures*, we saw how to make a test function with the #[test] attribute. Let us create a `test_eq` macro that generates a test function when it is invoked with this:

```
test_eq!(seven_times_six_is_forty_two, 7 * 6, 42);
```

The test function is as follows:

```
#[test]
fn seven_times_six_is_forty_two() {
    assert_eq!(7 * 6, 42);
}
```

We also want a test that fails:

```
test_eq!(seven_times_six_is_not_forty_three, 7 * 6, 43);
```

The first argument of `test_eq` is the test's name and the second and third arguments are values to be compared for equality, so in general, the format is: `test_eq!(name, left, right);`.

Here, `name` is an identifier; `left` and `right` are expressions. Like the `create_fn` invocation, the `test_eq!` calls are written outside a function.

Now, we can compose our macro as follows:

```
macro_rules! test_eq {
    ($name:ident, $left:expr, $right:expr) => {
        #[test]
        fn $name() {
            assert_eq!($left, $right);
        }
    }
}
```

You can create the test runner by calling `rustc --test macros.rs`.

When the macros executable is run, it prints out:

```
running 2 tests
test seven_times_six_is_forty_two ... ok
test seven_times_six_is_not_forty_three ... FAILED
```

A macro can also be recursive and call itself in the expansion branch. This is useful for processing tree-structured input, for example, when parsing HTML code.

Using macros from crates

As we demonstrated at the end of the *Adding external crates to a project* section, loading all the macros from an external crate should done by preceding the extern crate abc with the #[macro_use] attribute. If you only need the mac1 and mac2 macros, you can write this:

```
#[macro_use(mac1, mac2)]
extern crate abc;
```

If the attribute is not present, no macros are loaded from abc. Moreover, inside the abc module, only macros defined with the #[macro_export] attribute can be loaded in another module. To distinguish macros with the same name in different modules, use the $crate variable in the macro. Within the code of a macro imported from an abc crate, the special $crate macro variable will expand to ::abc.

Summary

In this chapter, we learned how to structure modules into crates to make our code more flexible and modular. Now, you also know the basic rules for writing macros for more compact and less repetitive code.

In the following chapter, we will explore the power of Rust when it comes to the concurrent and parallel execution of code, and how Rust also preserves memory safety in this area.

8
Concurrency and Parallelism

As a modern systems-level programming language, Rust has to have a good story for executing code concurrently and parallely on many processors simultaneously. And indeed, it does; Rust provides a wide selection of concurrency and parallel tools. Its type system is strong enough to write concurrent primitives that have properties unlike anything that existed before. Particularly, it can encode a wide selection of memory safe parallel abstractions that are also guaranteed to be data-race free while not employing a garbage collector. This is mind blowing as no other language can do this. All these features are not ingrained in the language itself, but they are provided by libraries, so improved or new versions can always be built. Developers should choose the tool that is right for the job at hand, or they can improve on or develop new tools.

We will discuss the following topics in this chapter:

- Concurrency and threads
- Shared mutable state
- Communication through channels
- Synchronous and asynchronous communication

Concurrency and threads

A system is concurrent when several computations are being executed at the same time and are potentially interacting with each other. The computations can only run in parallel (that is, simultaneously) when they are being executed on different cores or processors.

An executing Rust program consists of a collection of native operating system (OS) threads; the OS is also responsible for their scheduling. The unit of computation in Rust is called a `thread`, which is a type that is defined in the `std::thread` module. Each thread has its own stack and local state.

Until now, our Rust programs only had one thread, the `main` thread, corresponding with the execution of the `main()` function. However, a Rust program can create lots of threads to work simultaneously when this is needed. Each thread (not only `main()`) can act as a parent and generate any number of child threads.

The following action can be done on the data:

- It can be shared across threads (refer to the *Shared mutable state through atomic types* section)

- It can be sent between threads (refer to the *Communication through channels* section)

Creating threads

A `thread` can be created by spawning it; this creates an independent detached child thread that can generally outlive its parent. This is demonstrated in the following code snippet:

```
// code from Chapter 8/code/thread_spawn.rs:
use std::thread;
fn main() {
    thread::spawn(move || {
    println!("Hello from the goblin in the spawned thread!");
    });
}
```

The `spawn` argument is a closure (here without parameters, so `||`), which is scheduled to execute independently from the parent (here, this is the `main()`) thread. Note that this is a moving closure, which takes ownership of the variables in context. Our closure here is a simple print statement, but in a real example, this could be replaced by a heavy and/or time-consuming operation.

However, when we execute this code, we normally don't see any output; why does this happen? It turns out that `main()` is a bad parent (as far as threading is concerned) and doesn't wait for its children to end properly; when the end of `main()` shuts down the program, it terminates other threads even if they are still running. The output of the spawned thread becomes visible if we let `main()` pause for a brief moment before it terminates. This can be done with the `thread::sleep_ms` method, which takes an unsigned 32-bit integer in milliseconds:

```
fn main() {
    thread::spawn(move || { ... });
    thread::sleep_ms(50);
}
```

This now prints out: `Hello from the goblin in the spawned thread!`.

In general, this period of pause is not needed; children threads that are spawned can live longer than their parent thread and continue to execute when their parent has already stopped.

A better practice in this case, however, is to capture the join handle that `spawn` returns in a variable. Calling the `join()` method on `handle` will block the parent thread and make it wait until the child thread has finished its execution. It returns a `Result` instance; `unwrap()` will take the value from `Ok` and return the result of the child thread (which is `()` in this case because it is a print statement) or panic in the `Err` case:

```
fn main() {
  let handle = thread::spawn(move || {
      println!("Hello from the goblin in the spawned thread!");
  });
// do other work in the meantime
  let output = handle.join().unwrap();
  println!("{:?}", output); // ()
}
```

If no other work has to be done while the child thread is executing, we can also write this:

```
thread::spawn(move || {
// work done in child thread
}).join();
```

In this case, we are waiting synchronously for the child thread to finish, so there is no good reason to start a new thread.

Starting a number of threads

Each thread has its own stack and local state, and by default, no data is shared between threads unless it is immutable data. Generating threads is a very lightweight process since starting tens of thousands of threads only takes a few seconds. The following program does just that and prints out the numbers from 0 to 9,999:

```
// code from Chapter 8/code/many_threads.rs:
use std::thread;
static NTHREADS: i32 = 10000;
fn main() {
    for i in 0..NTHREADS {
        let _ = thread::spawn(move || {
```

```
        println!("this is thread number {}", i)
    });
  }
}
```

Since the numbers are printed in independent threads, the order is not preserved in the output; so, for example, it could start with:

```
this is thread number 1
this is thread number 3
this is thread number 4
this is thread number 2
this is thread number 6
this is thread number 5
this is thread number 0
...
```

A question that often arises is: how many threads do I have to spawn? The basic rule is that CPU-intensive tasks have the same number of threads as CPU cores. This number can be retrieved in Rust by using the num_cpus crate. Let's make a new project with cargo new many_threads --bin:

- Add the crate dependency to Cargo.toml:

  ```
  [dependencies]
  num_cpus = "*"
  ```

- Then, change main.rs to the following code:

  ```
  extern crate num_cpus;
  fn main() {
    let ncpus = num_cpus::get();
    println!("The number of cpus in this machine is: {}", ncpus);
  }
  ```

- From within the many_threads folder, do a cargo build to install the crate and compile the code. Executing the program with cargo run gives the following output (dependent on the computer): The number of cpus in this machine is: 8.

Now, you can start this (or any other) number of threads in a pool. This functionality is provided by the threadpool crate, which we can get by adding the threadpool = "*" to the Cargo.toml dependency and doing a cargo build. Add the following code to the start of the file:

```
extern crate threadpool;

use std::thread;
use threadpool::ThreadPool;
```

And, this code to the `main()` function:

```
let pool = ThreadPool::new(ncpus);
for i in 0..ncpus {
    pool.execute(move || {
        println!("this is thread number {}", i)
    });
}
thread::sleep_ms(50);
```

When executed, the preceding code yields the following output:

```
this is thread number 0
this is thread number 5
this is thread number 7
this is thread number 3
this is thread number 4
this is thread number 1
this is thread number 6
this is thread number 2
```

A thread pool is used for running a number of jobs on a fixed set of parallel worker threads; it creates the given number of worker threads and replenishes the pool if any thread panics.

Panicking threads

What happens when one of the spawned threads gets into a panic? This causes no problem as the threads are isolated from each other; only the panicking thread will crash after it frees its resources, but the parent thread is not affected. In fact, the parent can test the `is_err` return value from spawn as follows:

```
// code from Chapter 8/code/panic_thread.rs:
use std::thread;
fn main() {
  let result = thread::spawn(move || {
      panic!("I have fallen into an unrecoverable trap!");
  }).join();
  if result.is_err() {
   println!("This child has panicked");
  }
}
```

The preceding code prints out:

```
thread '<unnamed>' panicked at 'I' have fallen into an unrecoverable
trap!'
This child has panicked
```

Otherwise, to put it another way, the thread is the unit of failure isolation.

Thread-safety

Traditional programming with threads is very difficult to get right if you allow the different threads to work on the same mutable data, the so-called shared memory. When two or more threads simultaneously change data, then data corruption (also called data racing) can occur due to the unpredictability of the threads' scheduling. In general, data (or a type) is said to be thread-safe when its contents will not be corrupted by the execution of different threads. Other languages offer no such help, but the Rust compiler simply forbids non thread-safe situations to occur. The same ownership strategy that pervades Rust to prevent memory safety errors also makes you write safe concurrent programs. Consider the following program:

```
// code from Chapter 8/code/not_shared.rs:
use std::thread;
fn main() {
    let mut health = 12;
    for i in 2..5 {
        thread::spawn(move || {
            health *= i;
        });
    }
    thread::sleep_ms(2000);
    println!("{}", health); // 12
}
```

Our initial `health` is 12, but there are 3 fairies who can double, triple, and quadruple our health. We let each of them do this in a different thread, and after the threads are finished, we expect a `health` of 288 (which equates to 12 * 2 * 3 * 4). However, after their magical actions, our `health` is still at 12, even if we wait long enough to ensure that the threads are finished. Clearly, the three threads worked on a copy of our variable and not on the variable itself. Rust does not allow the `health` variable to be shared among the threads to prevent data corruption. In the next section, we will explore how we can use mutable variables that are shared between threads.

The shared mutable state

So, how can we make the `not_shared.rs` program give us the correct result? Rust provides tools, the so-called atomic types from the `std::sync::atomic` submodule, to handle shared mutable state safely. In order to share data, you need to wrap the data in some of the sync primitives, such as `Arc`, `Mutex`, `RwLock`, `AtomicUSize`, and so on.

Basically, the principle of locking is used, which is similar to that used by operating systems and database systems—exclusive access to a resource is given to the thread that has obtained a lock (which is also called a `mutex` and comes from mutually exclusive) on the resource. A lock can only be obtained by one thread at a time. In this way, two threads cannot change this resource at the same time, so no data races can occur; locking atomicity is enforced when required. When the thread that has acquired the lock has done its work, the lock is removed and another thread can then work with the data. In Rust, this is done with the generic `Mutex<T>` type from the `std::sync` module; sync comes from synchronize, which is exactly what we want to do with our threads. The `Mutex` ensures that only one thread can change the contents of our data at a time. We must make an instance of this type by wrapping our data as follows:

```
// code from Chapter 8/code/thread_safe.rs:
let data = Mutex::new(health);
```

Now, within the `for` loop, immediately after we spawn the new thread, we place a lock on the `health` object:

```
for i in 2..5 {
   thread::spawn(move || {
        let mut health = data.lock().unwrap();
        // do other things
   }
}
```

The call to `lock()` will return a reference to the value inside the `Mutex` and block any other calls to `lock()` until that reference goes out of scope, which will happen at the end of the thread closure. Then, the thread does its work and the lock is automatically removed. However, we still get an error: `capture of moved value: 'data'` message. This means that data cannot be moved to another thread multiple times.

This problem can be solved by using an equivalent of the `Rc` pointer from the *Reference counting* section of *Chapter 6, Pointers and Memory Safety*. Indeed, the situation here is very similar; all the threads need a reference to the same data, which is our health variable. So, we apply the same techniques from *Chapter 6, Pointers and Memory Safety* here—we make an `Rc` pointer to our data, and then we make a `clone()` of the pointer for each reference that is needed. However, a simple `Rc` pointer is not thread-safe; therefore, we need a special version of it that is thread-safe, the so called atomic reference counted pointer or `Arc<T>`. Atomic means that it is safe across threads, and it is also generic. So, we envelop our health variable inside an `Arc` pointer as follows:

```
let data = Arc::new(Mutex::new(health));
```

And, in the `for` loop, we make a new pointer to the `Mutex` with `clone`:

```
for i in 2..5 {
    let mutex = data.clone();
    thread::spawn(move || {
        let mut health = mutex.lock().unwrap();
        *health *= i;
    });
}
```

So, each thread now works with a copy of the pointer obtained by `clone()`. The `Arc` instance will keep track of the number of references to `health`. A call to `clone()` will increment the reference count on health. The `mutex` reference goes out of scope at the end of the thread closure, which will decrement the reference count. `Arc` will free the associated health resource when that reference count becomes zero.

Calling `lock()` gives the active thread exclusive access to the data. In principle, acquiring the lock might fail, so it returns a `Result<T, E>` object. In the preceding code, we assume that everything is okay. The `unwrap()` function is a quick means to return a reference to the data, but in the case of a failure, it panics.

Quite a few steps were involved here. So, we will repeat the code in its entirety again, but this time, we will provide robust error handling by replacing `unwrap()`. Digest each line with the explanations explained earlier:

```
// code from Chapter 8/code/thread_safe.rs:
use std::thread;
use std::sync::{Arc, Mutex};
fn main() {
  let mut health = 12;
  println!("health before: {:?}", health);
  let data = Arc::new(Mutex::new(health));
  tor i in 2..5 {
```

```
        let mutex = data.clone();
        thread::spawn(move || {
            let health = mutex.lock();
            match health {
                // health is multiplied by i:
                Ok(mut health) => *health *= i,
                Err(str) => println!("{}", str)
            }
        }).join().unwrap();
    };
    health = *data.lock().unwrap();
    println!("health after: {:?}", health);
}
```

This prints out:

```
health before: 12
health after: 288
```

(288 is indeed equal to 12 * 2 * 3 * 4). We join the threads to give them time to do their work; data is a reference, so we need to dereference it to obtain the health value:

```
health = *data.lock().unwrap();
```

The mechanism outlined in the preceding section using a combined Mutex and Arc is advisable when the shared data occupies a significant amount of memory; this is because with an Arc, the data will no longer be copied for each thread. The Arc acts as a reference to the shared data and only this reference is shared and cloned.

The Sync trait

An Arc<T> object implements the Sync trait (while Rc does not), which indicates to the compiler that it is safe to use concurrently with multiple threads. Any data that has to be shared simultaneously among threads must implement the Sync trait. A T type is Sync if there is no possibility of data races when the &T references are passed between threads; in short &T is thread-safe. All simple types such as the integer and floating point types are Sync, as well as all composite types (such as structs, enums, and tuples) built with simple types; any type that only contains things that implement Sync is automatically Sync.

Communication through channels

Data can also be exchanged between threads by passing messages among them. This is implemented in Rust by channels, which are like unidirectional pipes that connect two threads — data is processed first-in, first-out. Data flows over this channel between two end-points, from the `Sender<T>` to the `Receiver<T>`; both are generic and take the `T` type of the message to transfer (which obviously must be the same for the `Sender` and `Receiver` channels). In this mechanism, a copy of the data to be shared is made for the receiving thread, so you shouldn't use this for very large data:

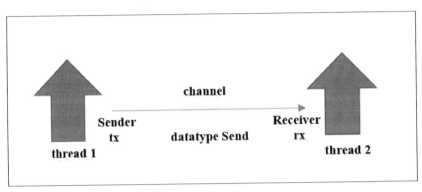

To create a channel, we need to import the `mpsc` submodule from `std::sync` (`mpsc` stands for **multi-producer, single-consumer communication primitives**) and then use the `channel()` method:

```
// code from Chapter 8/code/channels.rs:
use std::thread;
use std::sync::mpsc::channel;
use std::sync::mpsc::{Sender, Receiver};
fn main() {
   let (tx, rx): (Sender<i32>, Receiver<i32>) = channel();
}
```

This creates a tuple of endpoints; `tx` (t from transmission) is the `Sender` and `rx` (r from receiver) is the `Receiver`. We have indicated that we will send `i32` integers over the channel, but the type annotations are not needed if the compiler can deduce the channel's data type from the rest of the code.

Sending and receiving data

So, which data types can be sent over a channel? Rust imposes the requirement that data to be sent over a channel must implement the Send trait, which guarantees the safe transfer of ownership between threads. Data that does not implement Send cannot leave the current thread. An i32 is Send because we can make a copy, so let's do that in the following code snippet:

```
fn main() {
    let (tx, rx) = channel();
    thread::spawn(move|| {
        tx.send(10).unwrap();
    });
    let res = rx.recv().unwrap();
    println!("{:?}", res);
}
```

This, of course, prints 10.

Here, tx is moved inside the closure. A better way to write tx.send(10).unwrap() is as follows:

```
tx.send(10).ok().expect("Unable to send message");
```

This will ensure that, in case of a problem, a message is sent.

The send() is executed by the child thread; it queues a message (a data value; here, it is 10) in the channel and does not block. The recv() is done by the parent thread; it picks a message from the channel and blocks the current thread if there are no messages available. (If you need to do this in a non-blocking fashion, use try_recv().) If you don't process the received value, this blocking can be written as follows:

```
let _ = rx.recv();
```

The send() and recv() operations return a Result, which can be of the Ok(value) type or an Err error. Full error-handling is omitted here because in the case of Err, the channel does not work anymore, and it is better for the thread to fail (panic) and stop.

In a general scenario, we could make a child thread execute a long computation and then receive the result in the parent thread as follows:

```
// code from Chapter 8/code/channels2.rs:
use std::thread;
use std::sync::mpsc::channel;
fn main() {
    let (tx, rx) = channel();
```

```
    thread::spawn(move|| {
        let result = some_expensive_computation();
        tx.send(result).ok().expect("Unable to send message");
    });
    some_other_expensive_computation();
    let result = rx.recv();
    println!("{:?}", result);
}
fn some_expensive_computation() -> i32 { 1 }
fn some_other_expensive_computation() { }
```

The `result` function here has the `Ok(1)` value.

An elegant code pattern is shown in the following code snippet where the channel is created in a `make_chan()` function, which returns the receiving endpoint for the calling code:

```
// code from Chapter 8/code/make_channel.rs:
use std::sync::mpsc::channel;
use std::sync::mpsc::Receiver;
fn make_chan() -> Receiver<i32> {
    let (tx, rx) = channel();
    tx.send(7).unwrap();
    rx
}

fn main() {
    let rx = make_chan();
    if let Some(msg) = rx.recv().ok() {
        println!("received message {}", msg);
    };
}
```

This prints out: `received message 7`.

Perform the following exercise:

Construct a `shared_channel.rs` program that lets any number of threads share a channel to send in a value and has one receiver that collects all the values. As a hint, use `clone()` to give each thread access to the sending `tx` endpoint. (Refer to the example code in `Chapter 8/exercises/shared_channel.rs`.)

Synchronous and asynchronous communication

The kind of sending channel we used until now is asynchronous; this means that it does not block the executing code. Rust also has a synchronous channel type called sync_channel where the send() blocks if its internal buffer becomes full—it waits until the parent thread starts receiving the data. In the following code, this type of channel is used to send a value of the Msg struct over the channel:

```
// code from Chapter 8/code/sync_channel.rs:
use std::sync::mpsc::sync_channel;
use std::thread;
type TokenType = i32;
struct Msg {
    typ: TokenType,
    val: String,
}

fn main() {
    let (tx, rx) = sync_channel(1); // buffer size 1
    tx.send(Msg {typ: 42, val: "Rust is cool".to_string()}).unwrap();
    println!("message 1 is sent");
    thread::spawn(move|| {
    tx.send(Msg {typ: 43, val: "Rust is still cool".to_string()}).
    unwrap();
        println!("message 2 is sent");
    });
    println!("Waiting for 3 seconds ...");
    thread::sleep_ms(3000);
    if let Some(msg) = rx.recv().ok() {
      println!("received message of type {} and val {}", msg.typ, msg.
val);
    };
    if let Some(msg) = rx.recv().ok() {
      println!("received second message of type {} and val {}", msg.
typ, msg.val);
    };
}
```

Which prints:

```
message 1 is sent
Waiting for 3 seconds
```

Then, after 3 seconds, prints:

```
received message of type 42 and val Rust is cool
message 2 is sent
received second message of type 43 and val Rust is still cool
```

This clearly shows that the second message could only be sent when the buffer was emptied by receiving the first message.

Perform the following exercise:

Explain what happens when the second message is also sent from within the main thread and not in a separate thread.

Summary

In this chapter, we explored Rust's lightweight thread processes — how to create them, how to let them share data, and how to let them pass data through channels.

In the following chapter, we will have a look at the boundaries — we will see how a Rust program can take arguments to work with them. We will also examine what we have to do in Rust when we go to so such a low level that the compiler cannot guarantee safety anymore and how we can interface with other languages such as C.

9
Programming at the Boundaries

In this chapter, we look at how we can start up a Rust program with command-line parameters. Then, we go on to look at situations where we have to leave the safety boundaries, such as when interfacing with C programs, and how Rust minimizes potential dangers when doing so.

We will discuss the following topics:

- Program arguments
- Unsafe code
- Raw pointers
- Interfacing with C
- Inlining assembly code
- Calling Rust from other languages

Program arguments

Reading program parameters from the command line at startup is easy in Rust; just use the `std::env::args()` method. We can collect these parameters into a vector of `String` like this:

```
// code from Chapter 9/code/arguments.rs:
use std::env;

fn main() {
    let args: Vec<String> = env::args().collect();
    println!("The program's name is: {}", args[0]);
```

```
    for arg in args.iter() {
        println!("Next argument is: {}", arg)
    }
    println!("I got {:?} arguments: {:?}.", args.len() - 1);
    for n in 1..args.len() {
        println!("The {}th argument is {}", n, args[n]);
    }
}
```

Call the program in the following format:

- `arguments arg1 arg2` on Windows

- `./arguments arg1 arg2` on Linux and Mac OS X

The following is the output from a real call:

```
f:\>arguments Merlin Gandalf Sauron
The program's name is: arguments
Next argument is: arguments
Next argument is: Merlin
Next argument is: Gandalf
Next argument is: Sauron
I got 3 arguments:
The 1th argument is Merlin
The 2th argument is Gandalf
The 3th argument is Sauron
```

The program's name is `args[0]`; the next arguments are the command-line parameters. We can iterate through the arguments or access them by index. The number of parameters is given by `args.len() - 1`.

For more complex parsing with options and flags, use the `getopts` or `docopt` crate. To get started, there is an example at `http://rustbyexample.com/arg/getopts.html`.

Now, `env::vars()` returns the operating system's environment variables:

```
let osvars = env::vars();
for (key, value) in osvars {
        println!("{}: {}", key, value);
}
```

This starts with printing out the following on Windows:

`HOMEDRIVE: C:`

`USERNAME: CVO`

`LOGONSERVER: \\MicrosoftAccount`

...

Unsafe code

There are situations in which even the Rust compiler cannot guarantee us that our code will behave in a safe manner. This can occur in the following scenarios:

- When we have to program against the "metal", close to the operating system, processors, and hardware
- When we want to work with the same amount of control that is possible in C
- When we delegate a part of program execution to an unsafe language such as C
- When we want to inline assembly language

Rust allows us to code for these scenarios, but we have to envelop this possibly dangerous code in an `unsafe` block:

```
unsafe {
    // possibly dangerous code
}
```

Now, the programmer takes full responsibility. The `unsafe` block is a promise to the compiler that the unsafety will not leak out of the block. The compiler will check the code areas that are marked as `unsafe` more loosely and allow otherwise forbidden manipulations, but a number of rules from the ownership system (refer to *Chapter 6, Pointers and Memory Safety*, for more information) will still remain in place.

The clear advantage is that problem areas will now appear very well isolated; if a problem occurs, we will know that it can only occur in these marked code areas. Having a code base where 99 percent of the code is safe and 1 percent is unsafe is much easier to maintain than a code base with 100 percent unsafe code, as in C!

Here is what we can do in an `unsafe` block:

- Work with raw pointers, especially by dereferencing them. For more information, refer to the *Raw pointers* section of this chapter.
- Call a function in another language through a **Foreign Function Interface (FFI)**. For more information, see the *Interfacing with C* section of this chapter.
- Inline assembly code
- Use `std::mem::transmute` to convert simple types bitwise; here is an example of its use in which a string is transformed into a slice of bytes:

```
// code from Chapter 9/code/unsafe.rs:
use std::mem;
```

```
fn main() {
   let v: &[u8] = unsafe {
      mem::transmute("Gandalf")
   };
   println!("{:?}", v);
}
```

This prints the following output:

```
[71, 97, 110, 100, 97, 108, 102]
```

An unsafe block can also call the unsafe functions that perform these dangerous operations and are marked as unsafe fn dangerous() { }.

In unsafe code, the use of the std::mem module (which contains functions to work with memory at a low level) and the std::ptr module (which contains functions to work with raw pointers) is common.

 We recommend that you use assert! statements abundantly inside unsafe code to check at runtime whether it is doing what you expect it to. For instance, before dereferencing a raw ptr pointer of unknown origin, always call assert!(!ptr.is_null()); to ensure that the pointer points to a valid memory location.

Raw pointers

In unsafe code blocks, Rust allows the use of a new kind of pointers called *raw pointers*. For these pointers, there is no built-in security, and you can work with them with the same freedom as C pointers. They are written as follows:

- *const T: This is used for a pointer of an immutable value or the T type
- *mut T: This is used as a mutable pointer

They can point to invalid memory, and the memory resource needs to be manually freed. This means that a raw pointer could inadvertently be used after freeing the memory that it points to. In addition, multiple concurrent threads have nonexclusive access to mutable raw pointers. Since we're not sure of the contents (at least we have no compiler guarantee of valid content), dereferencing a raw pointer can also lead to program failure.

That's why dereferencing a raw pointer can only be done inside an `unsafe` block, as illustrated in the following code fragment:

```
// code from Chapter 9/code/raw_pointers.rs:
let p_raw: *const u32 = &10;
// let n = *p_raw; // compiler error!
unsafe {
    let n = *p_raw;
    println!("{}", n); // prints 10
}
```

If you try to do this in normal code, you will get the following output:

```
error: dereference of unsafe pointer requires unsafe function or block
[E0133]
```

We can make raw pointers safely out of references, implicitly or explicitly, with & as *const, as shown in the following snippet:

```
let gr: f32 = 1.618;
let p_imm: *const f32 = &gr as *const f32; // explicit cast
let mut m: f32 = 3.14;
let p_mut: *mut f32 = &mut m; // implicit cast
```

However, converting a raw pointer into a reference, which should be done through a &* (address of a dereference) operation, must be done within an `unsafe` block:

```
unsafe {
    let ref_imm: &f32 = &*p_imm;
    let ref_mut: &mut f32 = &mut *p_mut;
}
```

Raw pointers could also be useful when defining other more intelligent pointers; for example, they are used to implement the `Rc` and `Arc` pointer types.

Interfacing with C

Due to the vast functionality that exists in C's code, it can sometimes be useful to delegate processing to a C routine, instead of writing everything in Rust.

You can call all functions from the C standard library by using the `libc` crate, which must be obtained through Cargo. To do this, simply add the following to your Rust code:

```
#![feature(libc)]
extern crate libc;
```

To import C functions and types, you can sum them up like this:

```
use libc::{c_void, size_t, malloc, free};
```

Alternatively, you can use a * wildcard, such as use libc::*;, to make them all available.

To work with C (or another language) from Rust, you will have to use the FFI, which has its utilities in the std::ffi module.

Here is a simple example to call C for printing out a Rust string with the puts function in C:

```
// code from Chapter 9/code/calling_libc.rs:
#![feature(libc)]
extern crate libc;
use libc::puts;
use std::ffi::CString;

fn main() {
    let sentence = "Merlin is the greatest magician!";
    let to_print = CString::new(sentence).unwrap();
    unsafe {
        puts(to_print.as_ptr());
    }
}
```

This prints out the following sentence:

```
Merlin is the greatest magician!
```

The new() method of CString will produce a string (ending with a 0 byte) that is compatible with C from the Rust string. The as_ptr() method returns a pointer to this C string.

The #![feature(libc)] attribute (a so called feature gate) is (temporarily) necessary to enable the use of libc. It does not work with Rust from the beta channel, you need to take the Rust compiler from the nightly channel.

 Feature gates are common in Rust to enable the use of a certain functionality, but they are not available in stable Rust; they are only available in the current development branch (the nightly release).

Using a C library

Suppose we want to calculate the tangents of a complex number. The num crate offers basic operations on complex numbers, but at this time, the tangents function is not yet included, so we will call the ctanf function from the C library libm, which is a collection of mathematical functions that are implemented in C.

The following code does just that and defines a complex number as a simple struct:

```rust
// code from Chapter 9/code/calling_clibrary.rs:
#[repr(C)]
#[derive(Copy, Clone)]
#[derive(Debug)]
struct Complex {
    re: f32,
    im: f32,
}

#[link(name = "m")]
extern {
    fn ctanf(z: Complex) -> Complex;
}

fn tan(z: Complex) -> Complex {
    unsafe { ctanf(z) }
}

fn main() {
    let z = Complex { re: -1., im: 1. }; // z is -1 + i
    let z_tan = tan(z);
    println!("the tangens of {:?} is {:?}", z, z_tan);
}
```

This program prints the following output:

```
the tangens of Complex { re: -1, im: 1 } is Complex { re: -0.271753, im:
1.083923 }
```

The #[derive(Debug)] attribute is necessary because we want to show the number in a {:?} format string. The #[derive(Copy, Clone)] attribute is needed because we want to use z in the println! statement, after we have moved it by calling ctanf(z). The function of #[repr(C)] is to reassure the compiler that the type we are passing to C is foreign function-safe, and it tells rustc to create struct with the same layout as C.

The signatures of the C functions that we want to use must be listed in an `extern {}` block. The compiler cannot check these signatures, so it is important to specify them accurately to make the correct bindings at runtime. This block can also declare global variables that are exported by C to use in Rust. They must be marked as `static` or `static mut`, for example, `static mut version: libc::c_int`.

The `extern` block must be preceded by a `#[link(name = "m")]` attribute to link the `libm` library. This instructs `rustc` to link to that native library so that symbols from that library are resolved.

The C call itself must evidently be done inside an `unsafe {}` block. This block is enveloped inside a `tan(z)` wrapper function, which only uses Rust types. This way this wrapper can be exposed as a safe interface, by hiding the unsafe calls and type conversions between Rust and C types, especially C pointers. When the C code returns a resource, the Rust code must contain destructors for these values to assure their memory release.

Inlining assembly code

In Rust, we can embed assembly code. This should be extremely rare, but we can think of situations where this might be useful, for example, when you have to get the utmost performance or very low-level control. However, the portability of your code and perhaps its stability are decreased when you do this. The Rust compiler will probably generate better assembly code than you could write, so it isn't worth the effort most of the time.

This feature is not yet enabled in Rust 1.0 on the stable release channel. To use this mechanism (or other unstable features) in the meantime, you have to use Rust from the master branch (which is the nightly release).

The mechanism works by using the `asm!` macro, like this example where we calculate b in the subtract function by calling assembly code:

```
// code from Chapter 9/code/asm.rs:
#![feature(asm)]

fn subtract(a: i32, b: i32) -> i32 {
    let sub: i32;
    unsafe {
        asm!("sub $2, $1; mov $1, $0"
        : "=r"(sub)
        : "r"(a), "r"(b)
```

```
            );
        }
        sub
    }

    fn main() {
        println!("{}", subtract(42, 7)) }
    }
```

This prints out the result as 35.

We can only use `asm!` with a so-called feature gate, which is `#![feature(asm)]` here.

The `asm!` macro has a number of parameters separated by `:`. The first is the assembly template, containing the assembly code as a string, then the output and input operands follow.

You can indicate the kind of processor your assembly code is meant to execute on with the `cfg` attribute and its `target_arch` value, for example:

```
#[cfg(any(target_arch = "x86", target_arch = "x86_64"))]
```

The compiler will then check whether you have specified valid assembly code for that processor.

For more detailed information about the use of `asm!`, refer to the *Inline Assembly* section of this chapter at `http://doc.rust-lang.org/book/unsafe.html`.

Calling Rust from other languages

A Rust code can be called from any language that can call C. However, the Rust library should have the `dylib` crate type value. When `rustfn1` is the Rust function to be called, this must be declared as follows:

```
#[no_mangle]
pub extern "C" fn rustfn1() { }
```

Here, `#[no_mangle]` serves to keep the function names plain and simple so that they are easier to link to. C exports the function to the outside world with the C calling convention.

Examples of calling Rust from C, Python, Haskell, and Node.js can be found in the article at `https://siciarz.net/24-days-of-rust-calling-rust-from-other-languages/`. Calling Rust from Perl and Julia is shown at `http://paul.woolcock.us/posts/rust-perl-julia-ffi.html`.

Summary

In this chapter, we showed you how to process parameters for your program that are read from the command line at startup. Then, we proceeded to unsafe territory where raw pointers point the way. We covered how to use assembly code, how to call C functions from Rust, and how to call Rust functions from other languages.

This chapter concludes our essential tour of Rust. In the *Appendix, Exploring Further*, that follows this chapter, we provide you with pointers (no pun intended!) to pursue your Rust journey.

Exploring Further

Rust is a very rich language. In this book, we did not discuss each and every concept of Rust, and also not in every detail. Here, we will talk about what has been left out and where the reader can find more information or details about the topics.

Stability of Rust and the standard library

The Rust 1.0 production version comes with a commitment for stability; if your code compiles on Rust stable 1.0, it will compile with Rust stable 1.x with no or minimal changes.

The development of Rust follows a train model with three release channels (nightly, beta, and stable), and every six weeks a new stable release will take place. Production users will prefer to stick with the stable branch. Every six weeks, a new beta version is published; this excludes all unstable code, so you know that if you are using beta or stable, your code will continue to compile. Simultaneously, the existing beta branch is promoted to be a stable release. The nightly channel is what you use if you want the latest changes and additions; it includes unstable features and libraries that may still change in backwards incompatible ways.

The vast majority of functionality in the standard library is now stable. For in-depth information, refer to the documentation at `http://doc.rust-lang.org/std/`.

The ecosystem of crates

There is a general tendency to move less-used or more experimental **Application Programming Interfaces (APIs)** out of the language and the standard library and into their own crates. An ever-growing ecosystem of crates for Rust is at your disposal at `https://crates.io/`, with over 2,000 crates in stock at the time of writing (May 2015).

At *Awesome Rust* (`https://github.com/kud1ing/awesome-rust`), you can find a curated list of Rust projects. This site only contains useful and stable projects and indicates whether they compile in the latest Rust version. In addition, it is worth to search *Rust Kit* (`http://rustkit.io/`), as well as the Rust-CI repository at `http://www.rust-ci.org/projects/`.

In general, it is advisable that you search for crates that are already available whenever you embark on a project that requires specific functionality. There is a good chance that a crate that conforms to your needs already exists, or perhaps, you can find some usable starting code upon which you can build what you exactly need.

Other resources for learning Rust

This book has nearly covered all the topics of the so-called Book (`http://doc.rust-lang.org/book/`), and sometimes, it even went beyond. Nevertheless, the Book on the Rust website can still be a good resource to find the latest information, together with the fine collection of Rust code examples at `http://rustbyexample.com/`, which can be reached through the `More examples` link on Rust's homepage. For the most complete, in-depth information, refer to the reference at `http://doc.rust-lang.org/reference.html`.

Asking questions or following and commenting on the discussions on Reddit (`https://www.reddit.com/r/rust`) and Stack Overflow (`https://stackoverflow.com/questions/tagged/rust`) can also help you. Last but not the least, when you have an urgent Rust question, you can chat with the friendly experts on the IRC channel at `https://client01.chat.mibbit.com/?server=irc.mozilla.org&channel=%23rust`.

A resource with coding guidelines on Rust can be found at `http://doc.rust-lang.org/nightly/style/`.

24 days of Rust is a highly recommended article series by Zbigniew Siciarz on a multitude of advanced Rust subjects; you can take a look at the index at `https://siciarz.net/24-days-of-rust-conclusion/`.

Files and databases

The standard library offers the `std::io::fs` module for filesystem manipulation:

- If you have to work with **comma separated values (CSV)** files, use one of the available crates, such as `simple_csv`, `csv`, or `xsv`. The articles at `https://siciarz.net/24-days-of-rust-csv/` can get you started.

- For working with **JSON** files, use a crate such as `rustc-serialize` or `json_macros`; start with reading the information at `https://siciarz.net/24-days-of-rust-working-json/`.

- For the **XML** format, there are plenty of possibilities, such as the `rust-xml` and the `xml-rs` crates.

For databases, there are crates available for working with the following technologies:

- SQLite3 (the `rust-sqlite` crate)
- **PostgreSQL** (the `postgres` and `r2d2_postgres` crates); get started using it with `https://siciarz.net/24-days-of-rust-postgres/`
- **MySQL** (the `mysql` crate)
- For **MongoDB**, there is the `mongo` crate, built by the MongoDB developers; for more information on this, go to `http://blog.mongodb.org/post/56426792420/introducing-the-mongodb-driver-for-the-rust`
- For **Redis**, there are the `redis`, `redis-rs`, or `rust-redis` crates; see `https://siciarz.net/24-days-of-rust-redis/` for a quick start
- If you are interested in **object relational mapper (ORM)** frameworks, look at the deuterium crate

Graphics and games

Its high performance and low-level capabilities make Rust an ideal choice in the field of graphics and games. Searching for graphics reveals bindings for OpenGL (with packages `gl-rs`, `glfw-sys`), Core Graphics (with packages `gfx`, `gdk`), and others.

On the game front, there are game engines for Piston and chipmunk 2D and bindings for SDL1, SDL2, and Allegro5. A crate for a simple 3D game engine is `kiss3d`. A number of physics (`ncollide`) and math (`nalgebra` and `cgmath-rs`) crates exist that can be of use here.

Web development

A general overview of the status in this domain can be found at `http://arewewebyet.com/`. The most advanced and stable crate for developing HTTP applications at this moment is hyper. It is fast and contains both an HTTP client and a server to build complex web applications. To get started with it, read the introductory article at `https://siciarz.net/24-days-of-rust-hyper/`.

The HTTP client libraries built on top of hyper are `rust-request` and `rest_client`. A new Rust HTTP Toolkit project is emerging under the name teepee (`http://teepee.rs/`). It looks promising, but it was in its infancy at the time of writing this book.

For web frameworks, the best usable project is iron. If you only need a light micro web framework, rustful could be your choice. If you need a **Representational State Transfer (REST)** framework, go for rustless. Another useful web framework, which is still under active development, is nickel (`http://nickel.rs/`).

And of course, you must not ignore the new servo browser that is emerging!

Furthermore, crates exist for a lot of other categories such as functional and embedded programming (`http://spin.atomicobject.com/2015/02/20/rust-language-c-embedded/`), data structures, image processing (the `image` crate), audio, compression, encoding and encryption (`rust-crypto` and `crypto`), regular expressions, parsing, hashing, tooling, testing, template engines, and so on. You can take a look at the Rust-CI repository or the Awesome Rust compilation; you can refer to the links in the *The ecosystem of crates* section to get an idea of what is available. Zinc (`http://zinc.rs/`) is an example of a project that uses Rust to write a code stack for processors (at the moment, for ARM).

This brings us to the end of our Rust journey in this book. We hope you enjoyed it as much as we enjoyed writing it. You now have a firm foundation to start developing using Rust. We also hope that this quick overview has shown you why Rust is a rising star in the software development world, and that you will use it in your projects. Join the Rust community and start using your coding talents. Perhaps we'll meet again in the Rust(un)iverse.

Index

ecosystem 153, 154
macros, using from 127
public interface, exporting 117, 118
URL 111
custom conditions
reference link 43

D

developer tools
about 13
Sublime Text 14
Don't Repeat Yourself (DRY) 122
dynamic dispatch
reference link 86

E

enums
about 58, 59
Option 59
Result 59
error handling
about 77
failures 78
panics 78
expressions 29, 30
external crates
adding, to project 118, 119
importing 115-117

F

failures 78
file hierarchy
importing 114, 115
Foreign Function Interface (FFI) 145
format! macro
URL 21
functional and embedded programming
URL 156
functions
about 39-41, 74-77
documenting 41, 42

G

generic data structures 74-77
getopts
URL 144
global constants
about 18-20
printing, with string interpolation 20, 21

H

heap 89
higher-order functions 67, 68

I

idea-rust plugin
reference link 15
input
obtaining, from console 60, 61
IRC channel
URL 154
iterators 70, 71

J

JSON files
URL 155
Just In Time (JIT) 6

L

learning resources, Rust
databases 154, 155
files 154, 155
games 155
graphics 155
on IRC channel, URL 154
on Reddit, URL 154
on Stack Overflow, URL 154
web development 155, 156
lifetime, of variable 90-92
literal strings 48
LLVM compiler framework
URL 4
looping 37-39

M

macros
about 121
developing 122, 123
need for 121, 122
new function, creating 124, 125
reference link 123
repetition 124
using, from crates 127
Markdown formatting syntax
URL 18
match 98, 99
matching patterns 62-64
metadata information 42
methods, on structs 79-81
modules
about 109
defining 111
importing 114
items, visibility 112, 113
MongoDB
URL 155
multi-producer 138

N

nickel
URL 156

O

object relational mapper (ORM) 155
OpenDNS
URL 6
operator overloading 87
Option enum 59
ownership 99-102

P

Package Control package
reference link 14
panics 78
pointers
about 89, 95, 107

PostgreSQL
URL 155
primitive types 22
project
external crates, adding to 118, 119

R

racer
URL 13-15
raw pointers 146, 147
Read-Evaluate-Print-Loop (REPL) 15
Reddit
URL 154
Redis
URL 155
ref 98, 99
reference counting 105, 106
references 89, 96-98
Representational State Transfer (REST) 156
Resource Acquisition Is Initialization (RAII)
URL 101
Result enum 59
Rust
about 1
advantages 2, 3
calling, from other languages 151
calling, references 151
characteristics 3-5
code examples, URL 154
coding guidelines, URL 154
comparing, with other languages 5
first program 8, 9
homepage, URL 154
installing 7
learning, resources 154
reference link, for code 15
stability 153
standard library 153
URL 2
URL, for downloading 7
URL, for source code 7
using 5, 6
variable type, checking 27, 28
variable type, conversions 27

rustc command 8
Rust-CI repository
  URL 154
Rust documentation
  consulting 23
  URL 23
rusti
  about 15
  reference link 15
Rust Kit
  URL 154
rust-netbeans plugin
  reference link 15
Rust program
  arguments 143, 144
  unsafe scenarios 145, 146
RustyCage plugin
  reference link 15

S

Servo
  about 6
  URL 6
shared mutable state
  about 135-137
  Sync trait 137
single-consumer communication
      primitives 138
Skylight
  URL 6
slices 53
stack 89
stack and heap memory
  about 30-33
  URL 30
Stack Overflow
  URL 154
standard library, Rust
  about 153
  URL 153
strings
  about 48
  and arrays 54, 55
  literal strings 48
  reference link 50
string slice 49

struct 56-58, 98, 99
Sublime Text
  URL 14
  using 14
Sync trait 137

T

teepee
  URL 156
testing
  about 43, 44
  with cargo 45
test module 119-121
threads
  about 129
  creating 130, 131
  panicking 133
  starting 131-133
thread-safety 134
Tilde
  URL 6
TOML format
  reference link 11
trait constraints
  using 84, 86
traits
  about 82-84
  reference link 84
tuples 55, 56

V

values
  about 22
  copying 93, 94
  immutable values 25
  mutable values 25, 26
  variables, binding to 23, 24
variable
  aliasing 28, 29
  binding, to values 23, 24
  conversions 27, 28
  scope 26, 27
  shadowing 26, 27
  type, checking 27, 28
vectors 52, 53

VisualRust plugin
  reference link 15

W

web development
  URL 155

Z

zinc
  URL 7

Thank you for buying
Rust Essentials

About Packt Publishing

Packt, pronounced 'packed', published its first book, *Mastering phpMyAdmin for Effective MySQL Management*, in April 2004, and subsequently continued to specialize in publishing highly focused books on specific technologies and solutions.

Our books and publications share the experiences of your fellow IT professionals in adapting and customizing today's systems, applications, and frameworks. Our solution-based books give you the knowledge and power to customize the software and technologies you're using to get the job done. Packt books are more specific and less general than the IT books you have seen in the past. Our unique business model allows us to bring you more focused information, giving you more of what you need to know, and less of what you don't.

Packt is a modern yet unique publishing company that focuses on producing quality, cutting-edge books for communities of developers, administrators, and newbies alike. For more information, please visit our website at www.packtpub.com.

About Packt Open Source

In 2010, Packt launched two new brands, Packt Open Source and Packt Enterprise, in order to continue its focus on specialization. This book is part of the Packt Open Source brand, home to books published on software built around open source licenses, and offering information to anybody from advanced developers to budding web designers. The Open Source brand also runs Packt's Open Source Royalty Scheme, by which Packt gives a royalty to each open source project about whose software a book is sold.

Writing for Packt

We welcome all inquiries from people who are interested in authoring. Book proposals should be sent to author@packtpub.com. If your book idea is still at an early stage and you would like to discuss it first before writing a formal book proposal, then please contact us; one of our commissioning editors will get in touch with you.

We're not just looking for published authors; if you have strong technical skills but no writing experience, our experienced editors can help you develop a writing career, or simply get some additional reward for your expertise.

Go Programming Blueprint

ISBN: 978-1-78398-802-0   Paperback: 274 pages

Build real-world, production-ready solutions in Go using cutting-edge technology and techniques

1. Learn to apply the nuances of the Go language, and get to know the open source community that surrounds it to implement a wide range of start-up quality projects.

2. Write interesting, and clever but simple code, and learn skills and techniques that are directly transferrable to your own projects.

3. Discover how to write code capable of delivering massive world-class scale performance and availability.

Mastering Concurrency in Go

ISBN: 978-1-78398-348-3   Paperback: 328 pages

Discover and harness Go's powerful concurrency features to develop and build fast, scalable network systems

1. Explore the core syntaxes and language features that enable concurrency in Go.

2. Understand when and where to use concurrency to keep data consistent and applications non-blocking, responsive, and reliable.

3. A practical approach to utilize application scaffolding to design highly-scalable programs that are deeply rooted in go routines and channels.

Please check **www.PacktPub.com** for information on our titles

Getting Started with C++
Audio Programming for Game
Development

ISBN: 978-1-84969-909-9   Paperback: 116 pages

A hands-on guide to audio programming in game development with the FMOD audio library and toolkit

1. Add audio to your game using FMOD and wrap it in your own code.

2. Understand the core concepts of audio programming and work with audio at different levels of abstraction.

3. Work with a technology that is widely considered to be the industry standard in audio middleware.

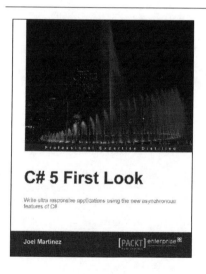

C# 5 First Look

ISBN: 978-1-84968-676-1   Paperback: 138 pages

Write ultra responsive applications using the new asynchronous features of C#

1. Learn about all the latest features of C#, including the asynchronous programming capabilities that promise to make apps ultra-responsive.

2. Examine how C# evolved over the years to be more expressive, easier to write, and how those early design decisions enabled future innovations.

3. Explore the language's bright future building applications for other platforms using the Mono Framework.

Please check **www.PacktPub.com** for information on our titles